EARTH SPIRIT

Belonging to the Earth

Nature Spirituality in a Changing World

EARTH SPIRIT

Belonging to the Earth

Nature Spirituality in a Changing World

Julie Brett

With contributions from
Jo Clancy, Kristoffer Hughes, David King, Bruce and
Patricia Shillingsworth, and Peter Williams

MOON
BOOKS
Winchester, UK
Washington, USA

JOHN HUNT PUBLISHING

First published by Moon Books, 2022
Moon Books is an imprint of John Hunt Publishing Ltd., No. 3 East Street, Alresford
Hampshire SO24 9EE, UK
office@jhpbooks.net
www.johnhuntpublishing.com
www.moon-books.net

For distributor details and how to order please visit the 'Ordering' section on our website.

ISBN: 978 1 78904 969 5
978 1 78904 970 1 (ebook)
Library of Congress Control Number: 2021944050

A CIP catalogue record for this book is available from the British Library.

Design: Matthew Greenfield

UK: Printed and bound by CPI Group (UK) Ltd, Croydon, CR0 4YY
Printed in North America by CPI GPS partners

We operate a distinctive and ethical publishing philosophy in
all areas of our business, from our global network of authors to
production and worldwide distribution.

Contents

Foreword 1

Acknowledgements 4

Introduction 6

Indigenous Cultures 11

Doing Better 14

More Than Words 19

Arriving Well Today – with *Peter Williams* 24

In This Together – with *Bruce* and *Patricia*
    Shillingsworth 32

The Elder Trees 39

We Belong to the Earth 42

The Land Speaks – with *Kristoffer Hughes* 47

Rituals of the Earth 51

The Earth Gorsedd 56

The Dam and The Gully – with *David King* 58

Layering the Wheel of the Year 64

Orality and Mnemonics 68

Dancing the Earth – with *Jo Clancy* 73

The Power of the Circle 79

Garden Life 83

Living Earth Wisdom 87

About the Author 89

Bibliography 90

Cover Art
Title: Leaf on the Track
Artist: Julie Brett

This is a close up of a leaf growing over the old Catalina Racetrack railings of The Gully *'Garguree'*, an important Aboriginal Place in Katoomba/Gedumba on Gundungurra Country. The Aboriginal community moved to Garguree from the Burragorang Valley after it was flooded to make way for the Warragamba Dam in 1948. In 1957 that same community was moved out to make way for a racetrack, but they fought this development hard for nearly 50 years, and eventually had it returned to their custodianship in 2002. They made a decision to leave the tarmac and metal railings of the racetrack there, and allow nature to slowly reclaim them, with moss, grasses and native plants growing over the roadway, rust slowly turning the metal back to Earth, and fungi reclaiming the wooden posts. This painting is a close up of the leaves on the plants growing over the road and railings: a reminder of the power of Mother Earth to reclaim what is hers and restore balance.

You must go
Into the forest
To hear 'revolution!'
Being whispered
By those
Who solemnly vow
To make a difference:
The bud
The rain
The soil
The sun
Go there and listen
For the change
You can become.
Julie Brett

Foreword

It is undoubtedly true that religions and communities in the past were in a far more intimate relationship with nature and the planet Earth, the home of every human that has ever lived, and precious because this fact is the one indissoluble bond that exists between all peoples and cultures, even those that seem to be irrevocably opposed. The twenty-first century may rightly be viewed as the last opportunity humanity has to right its relationship with nature, as the climate crisis worsens, and nation states struggle to make wise decisions that will secure a future for the next generation. There are many voices that should contribute to debates about planetary wellbeing and actions that could bring it about; those of scientists and citizens, politicians and workers, religious leaders and children, for example. Each of these groups is more varied than might be appreciated at first glance: factory hands and subsistence farmers are both "workers," but their worldviews differ markedly; environmentalists are political activists but unlike elected governments; and religious leaders include representatives of global religions like Christianity, Buddhism, and Islam, but also members of new faiths, and teachers from a plethora of Indigenous communities.

Julie Brett's *Belonging to the Earth: Nature Spirituality in a Changing World* casts its net more widely than her previous book, *Australian Druidry: Connecting with the Sacred Landscape* (2017), in that is deeply indebted to Indigenous Australian spirituality and the traditional elders who practice and teach these ancient ways in the contemporary world, and its message is broader than detailing how the path of Druidry, a tradition belonging to ancient and medieval Europe, can adapt to the radical otherness of the Australian landscape and its seasonal opposition to the northern hemisphere. The processes of healing and reparation between Indigenous Australians and settler Australians are

1

complex and multitudinous. Julie Brett's narrative draws upon her life story, born in England but brought up in Guringai Country on the Northern Beaches of Sydney, training as a Druid in Glastonbury, and living and working as an artist and spiritual author in Dharug and Gundungurra Country in the Blue Mountains west of Sydney. *Belonging to the Earth* is filled with stories and insights from Indigenous cultures, carefully connected to the specific lands and lore of each teacher and community Julie Brett met with and learned from in her travels and research to craft this book. It takes strength, courage, and sustained energy to contribute meaningfully to reconciliation between human cultures. Formal activities, such as the apology that the Labor Government made to the stolen generations, Indigenous people taken as children from their parents and cultures, on 13 February 2008, and the institution of National Sorry Day, which has been held on 26 May annually since 1998, play an important part. The personal communications that humans share are also ways to heal and to move forward. Protections enacted for the natural environment and celebration of Indigenous cultures are also valuable. Julie Brett moves from the environment to art, from Indigenous Australian traditions to her own Druidic practice, and from nature to culture and back again in a thoughtful meditation on what contemporary Australians can do to live their belonging to the Earth and craft pathways to the future that protect learning and lore, beauty and innovation, and that open up opportunities to develop new modes of living. The devastation wrought around the globe by bushfires, floods, the Covid-19 pandemic, and the gut-wrenching loss of tens of thousands of plant and animal species in the pursuit of industrial modernity should be a wake-up call to all. *Belonging to the Earth: Nature Spirituality in a Changing World* is a product of our times, and offers much to those seeking spiritual nourishment focused on bringing humans and nature back into an intimate relationship. Its timeliness, gentleness and good humour make it a pleasure for me to recommend this book.

Carole M. Cusack

University of Sydney

Acknowledgements

Firstly, I would like to acknowledge the Traditional Owners of the land that this book was written in, the place I call home, as the Dharug and Gundungurra people. I pay my respects to Elders past and present and express my deep gratitude for all that I have been able to learn here and with the wider Aboriginal community. I acknowledge the Traditional Owners of the many Countries I travelled through in researching this book, and thank every person who shared their story with me so that I might learn more about Aboriginal culture, community and experience. This beautiful land that I love so much always was, and always will be, Aboriginal land.

This book is the result of many journeys travelling around Australia and around my hometown, online and in person, through reading books and sharing rituals, meditations and moments of learning. I am grateful to everyone who was a part of that journey. Many thanks to Uncle Bruce Shillingsworth, Uncle Peter Williams and the other Elders who taught us so much on the Yaama Ngunna Baaka river festival tour, to Jo Clancy and her dance group in Wentworth Falls, to David King from the local Gundungurra Aboriginal community at The Gully 'Garguree', to Kristoffer Hughes of the Anglesey Druid Order in Wales, to friends in Druids Down Under, the Blue Mountains Organic Community Gardens, the Council of All Beings, to the many authors whose work has inspired me, to my wonderful family, and to everyone who walked this path with me as we wove these stories together.

The stories that follow are about our shared love for the Earth, her beauty and pain and the grief we feel when she is harmed. Some of these stories include explanations of things I have learned with Aboriginal friends and community in our joined experiences. Aboriginal stories are not mine to tell, so I have taken time whenever possible to share the words of Aboriginal community leaders after speaking with them about their stories and working to edit the chapters with them. When necessary, I have tried my best to explain key concepts using credible Aboriginal authors as sources of information. I have taken time to have the text checked by Aboriginal friends, however I know no one person can speak for all Aboriginal culture and there will be diversity of opinions, experiences, and even terminology. If there are any mistakes in my speaking about Aboriginal culture, they are my own responsibility, and as I learn more, I will take every step to do better in the future. My hope is that our shared love for the Earth will help us all to move forward together, always learning more.

Last but certainly not least, I give thanks to Mother Earth herself: the nurturing soil and stable stone beneath my feet; the life-giving waters that flow in the rain, rivers and seas; the fresh air I breathe and the voice of ancestors on the wind; the fiery warmth of the sun, and the warm core of the planet that keeps us all alive. Blessed are we all for being a part of you. May you thrive forever.

Introduction

We are a part of this world, our Mother Earth. We belong to her. It is right to feel like a part of a place rather than an impostor, drawing a line around what is human and what is 'natural' as though we are separate from the air we breathe, the ground we stand on, the soil that brings us food, the skies that rain down so that we might drink. We are the Earth. Everything we rely on to survive comes from nature. At times there is imbalance, sadness, grief, loss, or disconnection, but we can't be separated from the world. We are a part of these places, and they need us as much as we need them.

I have spent many years considering what it is to belong in a place. As a child the times I felt most at home in the world were when I was playing in the forest, climbing along the trunk of the big fallen palm tree by the waterfall at the end of our street; laying in the shallow creek waters that ran over red-orange rocks, surrounded by casuarina scrub and a dark blue summer sky; swimming in the waves at the beach as the sky turned pink and purple in the sunset; camping in the forest in winter, sitting by the fire, and looking at the stars at night. Nature was a place I felt I belonged.

In the world of humans and social interaction, I had not felt that belonging in quite the same way. I was born in England, but my family moved to Australia when I was six years old. We travelled back to England for holidays a few times through my childhood, to visit family mostly. Quite quickly England felt like the foreign place to me and I became an Australian, whatever that meant. Being Australian then was defined by an accent, certain words I used, and an inability to deal well with the cold. I knew little of history, or the ancient cultures of the land here. I was just a kid, playing in the bush and trying to make friends.

As I grew up, I was probably considered a bit weird for

paying close attention to nature and the seasons, but I found it exceedingly odd that no one had noticed certain patterns that happened every year. I found nature spirituality in my late teens and spent the next few years of my life exploring different paths and ideas until I came to Druidry, a modern nature-based spirituality inspired by what we know of the ancient Celtic Druids. It has been the core of my spiritual practice, but my influences are wider. I have also worked with the Wiccan community in Sydney and interstate, I have attended a Council of All Beings, and have a passion for learning about ecopsychology and its relationship to environmental activism.

These practices and paths have helped me to learn about what it is to belong to the land; to find alignment in ourselves with the seasons, the elements, and the environment around us, as well as the human stories of history, culture and art. Through these we come to discover who we are and how we belong to the world around us. We also find our responsibilities to the Earth.

In this book I am going to be sharing personal experiences of discovery, hope, healing and belonging: my own and those of friends I have met along the way. The stories will wind you through forest pathways, riversides and gardens, into ritual and dance, activism and art. I live a rambling life, following what is inspiring me and moving me to learn. These are the stories of those journeys and explorations of living in this changing world of ours, seeking answers, guidance and direction.

Some of the stories I share here are about my experiences with Aboriginal culture in Australia. I am certainly no authority on this information. I encourage you, whenever you can, please take the time yourself, to learn from First Nations people directly, and from the Elders in the Country you live in. This is relevant wherever you are in the world. Each place has stories and cultures that connect us with Mother Earth, and they should be supported, maintained and given deep respect. For those who are unfamiliar with First Nations cultures in Australia, please note that I use the titles 'Uncle' and 'Aunty' for some of the First Nations people interviewed in this book. This is used to show respect for Elders and I have done so when a person has been introduced to me in that way.

I personally identify with Pagan and neo-Pagan practices and communities. I call the path I walk 'Druidry' as many others do, as I am inspired to learn about my ancestral traditions of the British Isles. The ancient Celtic Druids were the spiritual leaders of the people living in ancient Britain, Ireland and parts of Europe. They were a part of a pre-Christian cultural tradition of ancestors and spirits, stories of nature and heroes, and an oral culture of poetic wisdom. Sadly, what we know of the ancient Druids is limited. They left no written records of their own, so our understandings of their beliefs and practices come to us through secondary sources. There was also systematic discrimination within Britain against Celtic language and culture for many years. People were prevented from speaking their language and passing on culture so it was done in secret. Thankfully this is changing in recent decades.

Despite the many years of difficulties faced by Celtic cultures, many places retained oral folk traditions and some practices and the old stories found their way into records of the Christian world. Many stories have survived in Wales, Ireland, and Scotland that are of vital importance to us today as we learn to recover these traditions. In England there are less pre-Christian examples than in the Celtic-speaking areas of Britain but some have survived in later folk tales. However, often those practicing modern Druidry turn to the older sources that have survived in the Celtic countries for inspiration and information. As such, it can be just as important for us, as English speakers, to consider cultural misrepresentation of these Celtic traditions as with any other Indigenous tradition. We learn with respect from those who speak Welsh, Irish and Scottish Gaelic when learning about these sources.

The word 'Pagan' comes from Latin *pāgānus*, meaning, 'rural' or 'rustic', and was originally used by the ancient Romans to delineate between the agricultural people and their traditions, and those of the city of Rome. Over time it also picked up the meaning of being against Christianity, but that is not how many of us who identify with the word see it today. Our traditions are very different to Christianity, and in some senses can be defined as 'Pagan' simply because they came before Christianity. We generally do not see them as opposed. They are just different. Personally, I see them as asking very different questions about the world. Pagan traditions are less concerned with moral structures and reward or punishment in the afterlife, instead they focus on our relationship with the land and our survival within it, the wisdom of poetry and art, stories of ancestors and heroes and magical beings, and mystery traditions that take us into the depths of what it means to be alive.

There are, of course, many forms of Christianity that honour nature and seek a path that is in harmony with the Earth. Some of the most brilliant writers on environmental connection are of a Christian background. We can work together. There is more that we share in our love for the Earth than what we disagree on in definitions of concepts. We learn from each other and support one another in our service to the health of the world around us.

That said, let me take a moment to explain terminology. In this book I use the term 'Pagan' and the term 'neo-Pagan' almost interchangeably as an umbrella term to refer to modern forms of Druidry and other nature-based traditions like Wicca, Heathenism, Asatru and others, but generally if I use 'neo-Pagan' I am referring to the more modern practices that have developed over the last few decades within these communities, as opposed to pre-Christian Pagan practices from which they are inspired. We do, however, refer to ourselves today as just 'Pagans' so there is a bit of back and forth in the text.

Today in Australia, Paganism is finding new acceptance after many years of discrimination. The last of the laws against Pagan practices were only lifted in 2008. Even so, many Pagans fear discrimination because of their beliefs even today. We are often misunderstood, or cast with negativity and fearful suspicion, but slowly we are finding more people understand us as traditions centred on a connection with nature and our ancestors. There are new opportunities arising for us to rediscover our heritage and the ways our ancestors connected with the Earth, and as understanding is found and discrimination is reduced.

Our traditions take us through journeys across the landscapes of our ancestors, showing us how to listen with respect to the lands we find ourselves on today. Practicing Druidry in Australia, we learn respect for local Indigenous cultures and First Nations people. We learn about local flora and fauna, local seasons and stories. We are discovering new ways of practicing here that honour both our own Celtic ancestors and the ancestors of the lands we live in.

What we share with the Indigenous cultures of Australia is an understanding that we are not separate from the Earth. The Earth holds us and we have a responsibility to care for her, wherever we are, whoever we are. Honouring our ancestors and the ancestors of the land on which we stand, we follow in the footsteps of those who walked the Earth more gently. In addition, we know that the state of the Earth reflects our inner selves. Our health and wellbeing are intricately and intrinsically linked to hers. In some ways, the world has lost touch with the wisdom of these traditions, and there is an urgency to come back and listen again, so that we can find our wholeness with the world around us, even as it shifts through times of pain and trouble. It is through recognising these struggles in the Earth, and in ourselves, that all of us will come to healing.

Indigenous cultures

The word 'indigenous' means to naturally occur in a place or country; in cultural terms it refers to the First People of a place; and in more intimate terms, it refers to people who are living in relationship with the land. In this book I use the term 'Indigenous' to emphasise cultural connections to specific places, but I understand that 'First Nations' is preferred by some people and have favoured it in some chapters. I mean no disrespect by using the term 'Indigenous' when I do. I hoped that in using it, I would be focusing on that incredibly important Earth-connection that so many First Nations cultures are built upon.

The word also relates to the term 'Indigenised thinking,' which is used to help all people understand what it is to live in close relationship with the land whether we identify as an Indigenous person or not. Robin Wall Kimmerer, a native American woman of the Potawatomi Nation, in her beautiful book *Braiding Sweetgrass* explains that:

"It was through her actions of reciprocity, the give and take with the land, that the original immigrant became indigenous. For all of us, becoming indigenous to a place means living as if your children's future mattered, to take care of the land as if our lives, both material and spiritual, depended on it."

It is vitally important for ourselves, and for the futures of generations to come, that we walk with respect towards Indigenous cultures of the First Nations peoples of the lands we are in, wherever we go, and whoever we are, and learn how we too can live in reciprocity and partnership with the lands we call home.

We live in a time in history where a huge proportion of the world's human population is living outside of the lands they are ancestrally and culturally indigenous to. A greater proportion than at any other time in history. Air travel, trains and cars have made it possible to fly to the other side of the planet and to any place we wish in a matter of days or hours: an inconceivable speed and distance in comparison to our ancestors. In times gone by, a greater proportion of humans were in intimate relationship with the land that they lived on and their identities were firmly aligned with place. The speed of travel today, and the integration of cultures all over the world, has made it more difficult for many of us to have that same sense of belonging to place that our indigenous ancestors would have had. Negotiating these changes is part of the work of our time and learning how to find our place in the world calls for a better understanding of connection to place.

Indigenous cultures of the world, both in the past, and today, are intimately entwined with knowledge of the resources, history, and stories of the land. Knowledge of plants, seasons, weather, food resources, sustainable management of hunting and fishing, fire management and the management of human relationships within that system of the environment make up the building blocks of Indigenous cultures. These are systems that work within specific spaces in relationship to specific lands. Culture is Indigenous in place and every place has a people.

I was brought up in Guringai Country on Sydney's Northern Beaches, and now live in Dharug and Gundungurra Country in the Upper Blue Mountains to the west of the city. My learning about Aboriginal culture has been slow and awkward over the years. There was a lot of guilt, confusion, misinformation, shyness, fear and naivety to overcome before I really started to learn. And I know I still stumble along tripping over myself and making mistakes as I go but learning all the same. All I can do is try to do better today. I feel I have come a long way, as has Australia as a whole, but there is still a long way to go.

We pay our respects to all Indigenous cultures, whether these are of our own ancestors or the land we stand on, or any of those who we hope to learn from. More than anything, Indigenous cultures need to be heard, supported and valued. We find this through building relationships, making friends, spending time together sharing what is important to us, and listening, always listening. Indigenous cultures hold the history of ancestors and their connection to place, and that cannot be underestimated in the journey we all face in adapting to a changing world. Making connections with others based on our shared value of these traditions and a hope for respectful understanding is integral to the healing of our world and our hearts, and our understanding of what it is to belong.

Doing Better

Do the best you can until you know better.
Then when you know better, do better.

Maya Angelou

'Doing better' is a phrase that I have come to use quite a lot. I want to act with integrity and sound ethics, but I also make mistakes and fumble along as I attempt to be a better person. Doing better is not a lofty goal of being perfect – it is a realistic goal that maybe today, I could do a bit better than I did yesterday. It holds an awareness of our human fallibility and the bumpy road we take to learning more. It is a phrase that has become increasingly important to me to understand how my own spiritual practice works in relation to Indigenous traditions, both those of my own ancestors, and those of the land I live in.

Doing better, means learning about Aboriginal culture and the expectations there are for us as people on stolen, unceded land. It asks us to act with respect and to take time to find out more about the First Nations cultures of the lands that we call home. It recognises that we might make mistakes, and that we want to learn more. It's gentle in that it knows this learning takes time.

It is a long learning journey for non-Aboriginal Australians to not only learn about Aboriginal culture, but to shift out of misunderstandings, projections and stereotypes we might not even be aware that we hold. It can take time and effort, and a long hard look at ourselves for many non-Aboriginal people to come to a position where we are really doing right by Aboriginal people. There is a lot to learn and to unlearn. I know I make mistakes as I learn to do better, but if we keep that as the goal – to always be trying to do better – we will make a difference.

In my last book, *Australian Druidry,* I included some information about honouring Indigenous wisdom, but I did not go into a great amount of detail about it. I briefly explained the need to acknowledge Country, respect the protocols around sacred sites, to credit stories to traditional owners and their countries, and seek out opportunities to learn about the local First Nations community, Country and history. One reason for not going into a great amount of detail is that I believe we should be learning from Indigenous people about these subjects. There are many fantastic authors sharing their stories and wisdom, and many communities that offer learning opportunities in person. There is probably one near where you live. The other reason is that I was really only at the beginning of my journey of learning and still needed a great deal of guidance myself. I am still learning and trying to do better myself. In this book I would like to address some topics in a little more detail because I think, in the context of Earth custodianship it would be a disservice to not talk about it. I hope I can do the explanation justice when my words are needed, but encourage you to supplement this by finding out more from your local First Nations community.

Here in Australia, one way that many of us try to do better with our rituals is to include an 'Acknowledgement of Country', or if we are able to, a Traditional Owner is asked to give a 'Welcome to Country'. It is important to know the difference. A Welcome to Country can only be performed by a Traditional Owner or Custodian of the country they are in. A 'Traditional Owner' is an Aboriginal person or Torres Strait Islander who is acknowledged by their community as being a direct descendent of the original custodians of a particular Country. An Aboriginal person is defined for this purpose someone who has Aboriginal family heritage, identifies as Aboriginal, and is accepted as Aboriginal by the Aboriginal community with which they are associated. This is similarly the case for Torres Strait Islanders. A Welcome to Country cannot be performed by anyone but a Traditional Owner in their own Country. They cannot perform a Welcome to Country in another part of Australia. This would be called an Acknowledgement of Country.

An Acknowledgement of Country can be done by anyone anywhere in Australia. Even an Aboriginal person in another Country would perform an Acknowledgement of Country rather than a Welcome to Country. This is very important to understand. If you are not Aboriginal, you will always be performing an Acknowledgement of Country no matter where you are.

An Acknowledgment of Country is given at the beginning of all kinds of events from council meetings, to school assemblies, to the opening of new public facilities, to awards ceremonies, fairs or other community gatherings. The more important an event is, or the more relevant to Aboriginal people it is, the more important it is to have a Traditional Owner give a Welcome to Country. If you are holding a large gathering and would like to include a Welcome to Country, you can contact your local First Nations led organisation to find out about asking a Traditional Owner to perform one for you. There is usually a payment for this.

If you are in Australia, you can include an Acknowledgement of Country in any small ritual, including one you do alone. An Acknowledgment of Country can be specific or non-specific depending on how much you know about the place you are holding your ritual. Find out what Country you are on in a few minutes with an internet search, even if you are out of your usual area of practice. You may find there are disputes over the land you are on, in which case you might like to consider wording that respectfully reflects that situation. If you are not in Australia you might like to find out what is appropriate where you live. How would the Indigenous people of your land like to be recognised? These small gestures can make a big difference.

Many Pagans here like to touch the earth as they do an Acknowledgement of Country, recognising the connection to the earth held by Indigenous cultures, but you may prefer to sit or stand. Here is an example of how to word a very simple

Acknowledgement of Country as either a solo ritualist, or in a small group.

Solo:
"I acknowledge the (country name) people as the Traditional Custodians of this land, where I hold my ritual today. I pay my respects to Elders, past and present."

Group:
"We acknowledge the (country name) people as the Traditional Custodians of this land where we hold our ritual today. We pay our respects to Elders, past and present, and extend that respect to any Aboriginal or Torres Strait Islander people with us today."

We are also encouraged here to add more about our personal feelings about the history of displacement for First Nations people; their connection to the land, waters and skies; the strength of culture; and the importance of sacred sites. The fact that the land was never ceded, and that Aboriginal people remain sovereign on their own land, are also phrases you can include. We have been asked to sit with the truth, with the land, and with what we know of the Country we are in and reflect on that in our Acknowledgement of Country. This can be a very healing practice.

It is important that our Acknowledgements of Country in ritual are not just rote procedure but are heartfelt. Each of us feels the sacredness of this land, its creatures, plants, spirits and stories, and acknowledging Indigenous cultures and their connection to these should be an important part of any Earth centred ritual. Let me explain this better with a story...

First Words

We walk in together, circling around the small ritual space we have created in the gardens by the creek. There is a big wattle tree shading us and a willow in the water. There are apple trees with perching cockatoos and tea tree bushes along the creek. The kookaburras are laughing in the big pine tree up the hill. Over the creek, the swampland is lined by lomandra longifolia and mountain ash eucalyptus trees. We walk past hazels and peach trees, waratahs and native indigo bushes as we make our way to the circle. The group has come together to honour the season in our small stone circle built of sandstone blocks. Eight stones mark the compass directions, the positions of sunrise and sunset, the elements and the seasonal festivals of the wheel of the year.

We gather into the space, walking sunwise (anticlockwise for us), as we find a place to stand, all facing inwards. We are silent and ground into the earth with our intention. We look and listen. We feel the breeze on our skin and smell the scents in the air. The first words of the ritual are spoken as many of us bend down to touch the earth:

"We stand today, on Dharug and Gundungurra land: land that was never ceded. We acknowledge the Dharug and Gundungurra people as the Traditional Owners of the land here: this place. We recognise their deep and abiding connection to the land, the waters and the skies; to the plants, animals, landforms, sacred sites and seasons. We acknowledge the sadness and suffering that has occurred here and express our sincere hope for reconciliation, for healing, and for the continued strength of the Dharug and Gundungurra people. We express our gratitude for their generosity in teaching us about this land and the community we have here. We pay our respects to Elders past and present and extend that respect to any Aboriginal and Torres Strait Islander people here today."

The ritual continues as we honour the season, find messages from the garden's mixture of native and introduced plants, and give our gratitude for life and the ways the seasons shape our journeys...

More than Words

Of course, words are not actions. Though speaking words of support and acknowledgement are powerful and can help us all to be reminded of the importance of Indigenous connections to the land, there are also many more concrete ways that we can support the strength of Indigenous cultures and, in times of climate crisis, those connections are important to us all.

I live in a town called Katoomba in Dharug and Gundungurra Country, a place also known as the Upper Blue Mountains of New South Wales in Australia. In 2019 we had a very dry year. I hardly remember using my umbrella at all and when I did use it, it was probably only used as a sunshade. The dams were low, especially worrying as we are on the edge of Sydney, the largest city in Australia. The drought had been tough. The ground almost rang with my footsteps; it was so dry. The grass all died back, and the garden was sand and dust. Water restrictions meant we couldn't use the hose at all. We could only water the garden with a watering can before 10am and after 4pm. A lot of the veggies were not coping well with the heat and intense sun with so little water.

The drought dragged on and on and I was concerned for the trees in our yard. I hooked up an extension pipe from our washing machine to a big bin out the back door and collected the water from washing the clothes so that I could get some water down to the trees at the front of our house. I switched to soap nuts, a natural washing agent, rather than detergent powders so that the water was good for the trees. I was truly worried they would die without this water from our laundry. It felt so precious. Not a drop of water was wasted in our house. We showered standing in a bucket so we could pour it out onto the lawn or onto the trees afterwards, and a shallow bucket was always in the sink so that water could be given to the plants too. Quite a few trees in the area did die that year. You could see them as you drive along the highway up the mountains. Skeletons in a sad forest. They simply died from a lack of water and never recovered. That year I started getting really worried about the environment. Climate rallies were in full swing. I marched, I followed Greta Thunberg on social media, I cried over the hundreds of thousands of hectares that burned in the Amazon rainforest. Then I saw the fish kills in the Menindee Lakes here in Australia and knew I had to do more than just sit and watch online and cry. I remember this moment, just looking at my screen, a video of a Rob McBride from Tolarno Station holding an ancient Murray cod nearly a metre long; he was gagging at the smell of its dead body and nearly in tears himself as he described how many of these ancient fish had died and how devastated the communities were about the mismanagement of the waterways. With tears in my own eyes, I watched and clicked to share, but at the same time it all seemed so far away, and was I really doing anything just clicking to share and feeling sad?

News at the time had been strange. There had been a lot of concern online over 'fake news' and it had caught me out a couple of times as I shared articles about deforestation that turned out to be reconstructed from old stories to create 'clickbait'. I felt a real need to take these experiences away from social media, and an urge to go and see it for myself. I knew what I needed to do was get off the computer and go see it face to face, so that I could find out how we can really make a difference. Sitting on the computer was not going to cut it anymore.

Not long afterwards, I found information about a trip out to see the rivers and to learn what was happening there and I jumped at the chance. The Yaama Ngunna Baaka (Welcome to our Rivers) corroboree tour was run by Uncle Bruce Shillingsworth, a Murrawari and Budjiti man, and his family along with First Nations river communities, with the support of environmental activist groups, local politicians and community groups working for change. For five days we travelled alongside the river together, from Walgett to Brewarrina, Bourke, Wilcannia and the Menindee Lakes.

At each place we learned about the local concerns for the river and local history, we met people who lived there, and heard about the local experiences of loss. We saw the bone dry, deep riverbeds, lakes and waterways. In the evening each day we gathered for a corroboree where First Nations' people performed dance, storytelling, song and ceremonies about the river and the land, its people and its creatures. It was heartbreaking to see the rivers so dry and barren and to learn about the difficulties the communities had been having, but it was also incredibly beautiful and eye-opening for so many of us to learn about Aboriginal culture in this way and to see how these ancient stories tell us so much about the ways the river can be managed for its health and for the health of everything and everyone that depends on it. Through this we learned about connecting to the land and the environment on a spiritual level as well a practical level.

Recently I went to a gallery opening night for an exhibition about the tour. Uncle Bruce explained to the audience there:

"The five communities, Walgett, Brewarrina, Bourke, Wilcannia, Menindee where we done the corroboree in 2019 are very special. The corroboree Yaama Ngunna Baaka is about bringing non-Indigenous people to the rivers, to our land, to our country, to sit with our Elders and to sit with the people of the land and to talk about the issues and the problems that affect all of us. It's about that river. It's about water. Water is life! Water feeds the land. Nothing ain't going to live without no water. So, all the cotton and the big agriculture now they're sucking our rivers, diverting our rivers, building huge dams and storing water. Where are First Nations' rights to water? Where's First Nations' rights? My people have been living on their land for thousands and thousands of years. Now they're forced to get off their lands and move to bigger towns and bigger cities. My people have been connected to the land for a long, long time. Our stories, our dance, they represent who we are. It's our identity."

As we went to each place on the tour, we were all welcomed and told that the First Nations people there felt a responsibility to care for everyone that came to their land, and to care for the land itself. As a non-Aboriginal person this touched me to the core. I had felt afraid before. I thought that I'd be told I wasn't welcome, that I had to go back to England, that I was an awful coloniser who shouldn't be there. But that wasn't the message I got at all. I only ever felt welcomed and cared for and that welcome was extended out to everyone. I made beautiful friendships grounded in a shared love for the Earth and for wanting justice for these beautiful communities and strength for their culture.

The histories of hardship and injustice were heartbreaking and at the beginning we did not know what to do about any of it, so we listened and we learned. We learned what kind of things we needed to ask the government to do – that they need to include the First Nations people in the decision-making process, because they understand the land. We learned about the people and the places we visited. They shared stories, songs and dances in the corroborees each night. The ritual of coming together to acknowledge the Traditional Owners and the Elders, and to tell the stories of the place; everyone coming together wanting hope and healing and a better life for this river and its communities – that was powerful, and it was clearer to me how things needed to change.

This was emphasised by the presence of activists, environmentalists and local farmers also coming to support the cause and to talk to us, educating us on the issues from several different perspectives. It was clear to all of us how important the

Aboriginal connections to the land are, and how we all just want the rivers to flow, and for these communities to thrive.

It was important to me to be there, in person, making these connections, listening, and learning first-hand. It was an action and not just words. It's one thing to sit on the computer and like or share a post on social media, or even to speak words of respect in our rituals. It's another to get out there and see these things for ourselves and to try to make a difference with our acts. Not only can we learn first-hand, we can also be of support by attending events, donating to First Nations communities and causes, purchasing goods and services from First Nations artists and businesses, educating ourselves by reading First Nations authors work, writing to our government representatives for change, and talking to friends about these important issues. Speaking words is one thing but taking action matters – making a difference with more than just words is work we all need to undertake.

Arriving Well Today
with Peter Williams

On the Yaama Ngunna Baaka tour I met Uncle Peter Williams. He is from the Brewarrina area, and was one of the leaders of song in the corroborees at the rivers. He calls the river the Parwon, rather than the Baaka, and has told me it has many names in Aboriginal languages as you move along from the source to the sea. Though he is from Garulgiyalu clan of the Ngiyampaa nation, he lives here in the same town as me in the mountains in Dharug and Gundungurra country.

In my curiosity to learn more about how people interested in nature-based spiritual practices could be more respectful towards Aboriginal culture, we got to talking. We started creating some notes to share with the Druidry community about it. I also found out that he also has Welsh and Scottish ancestry and was interested in learning a bit about what we do too. So, one day I sat down with him to talk about his story and his dreams for the future, and we recorded a conversation at my home.

"How should I introduce you?" I ask at the beginning

"Ah, just Peter's fine," replies Uncle Peter, but he's being very humble.

"I've heard you called a senior song..." I trail off wondering how to put it.

"A senior song person, yeah," He confirms.

We have had talks before about the trouble there can be with calling oneself an Elder. Claiming authority for oneself is often not particularly well received. It is better to have others name you in that way rather than doing it yourself, and I understand that is what he is alluding to when he frames this part of the conversation by saying,

"Too much responsibility," smiling and laughing it off.

Of course, Uncle Peter, just like any other Aboriginal person, can't speak for all Aboriginal people, just like I can't speak for all people practicing Druidry. We are individuals, we have opinions of our own, and sometimes our positions and ideas are just personal. There is diversity. He describes himself as having some "far-fetched" ideas when it comes to spiritual beliefs, but he also clearly stands strong in his traditional culture and is very well spoken of by others in his community and I have heard him referred to as an Elder, but there is caution there and deep respect in his hesitation. I ask him about how he began his journey doing what he does. He started learning the traditional ways in his 20's and explains:

"When Uncle Paul and Brother Ray was teaching us how to do our dances, oh, that was a wild time. They were hard on me, because I was the first of the rebuilding of dancing. Other than those two, because they're brilliant at everything. Once we started the ceremonies up, everything started to come with that, dancing, language, storytelling, being tour guides for our sites; so, I've been through the whole system with the old fellas."

He explains the story of learning and how in 2010 he and his family started getting involved with corroborees along the rivers that flow between Queensland and South Australia. He tells a little about the songline stories of the Kangaroo, Goanna, Echidna and Emu. These stories brought people together from across the land for celebrations in corroborees. He shares with me his journey of learning and teaching his culture with his family and community, and he tells me about the first time they got involved with the dancing at the river corroborees:

"The start of the river [a tributary to the Parwon] was about 80k's out of Cunnamulla heading east, so it was on a property there and that was our first dance. Then we came into Bre [Brewarrina] and we danced at the fish traps. That was spectacular. Of course, I'd never danced there before. That was pretty much my first time doing corroboree at the fish traps. The one before that was over at Bourke, at the Yamakara Festival, and for me and my daughter, my son-in-law, and my sons to dance there, with our language, it was like... the peak of dancing for me. And every night as we danced from Bre all the way to Coorong, we had a light sprinkle of rain without clouds, so that, for me, was telling us, it was right, everything was perfect."

For Uncle Peter, cultural artforms of each place bring the land back into balance. He explained that his priority is to see Aboriginal people learn about their own culture, and to reawaken the art, dance, stories and ceremonies of their own tribal areas and Countries. He explains that particular styles of art and culture belong to specific places and should be maintained in those places, and by the people who are from those places, as a part of culture. He has explained to me how he started out painting in dotting, x-ray, and crosshatching styles, but then learned that these come from specific places. Dot style art comes from the Central Desert regions, x-ray style is from Arnhem Land and Queensland, and crosshatching is also from Arnhem Land. He had then learned about the cave style of artwork from his own Ngiyampaa Country at places like Mount Gundabooka and Mount Grenfell and adjusted his art style to be more in line with the traditions of those places. He stressed a need for Aboriginal people as well as people from other places, to return to their roots of culture.

He explained how this is something that can happen on a global scale, with each country of the world returning to their local ancestral artforms of dance, art, music, song and ceremony to bring balance back to the land. He feels that this way of returning to the old ways of the ancestors isn't a turning back of time to old ways of being. It can be a part of our modern lives, but that the maintenance of those old cultures and their artforms should be a part of that modern life:

> "Every culture has got to go back to the old way, as far as I'm concerned. And the new stuff today [meaning modern life], it coincides with the old way, but it shouldn't change the old way. They can live together, but the old way has to be the old way."

He sees an importance in returning to the old ways as bringing healing to the whole of the planet, saying:

> "All the cultures all over the world are old and, you know, I'm not saying who's older than who or what comes first, but once we all get the designations back to where it was, with all the languages doing what they're doing, and the ceremonies in the right spaces, it's like the acupuncture points on our bodies. You do that for Mother Earth all over the world, and we're doing the acupuncture at the times they're supposed to be done, then this planet's going to just go from being in aftershock to being full back, because all the cultures are not doing what they're supposed to be doing."

I ask what he thinks the effect of that might be: "Well, Peter's concept is pretty far-fetched to everyone else's..." he laughs, and tells me his own take on it:

> "See, once Australia... once we get all the tribal areas back to doing ceremonies in their areas, it's like the pin cushion for mother earth, the songs, the land... Everyone else is taking from the land but no one is giving back, there's only a few pods in NSW that are doing ceremonies of sorts. Queensland is doing theirs, Western Australia, South Australia and the Northern Territory... they are into theirs still. Once everyone

gets ceremonies in their areas for the times we're supposed to have them, then you'll find the pulse will happen better. I say pulse because it's not just once we get Australia settled, with language and dance and ceremonies... the rest of the world has got to do their languages and ceremonies in their areas, and then just imagine a world pulse."

He imagines the world being healed though our all returning to the old ways of ceremony, bringing health back to the whole planet. I ask how myself and others like me, as people who are not from here can be a part of this. He says his opinion is "when in Rome" implying that when we are in Australia, we should be learning about the Aboriginal cultural practices. We talk about Uncle Peter's dreams to reawaken the corroborees in Brewarrina a few times a year as a way for people to come back to culture and learn. I ask if the festivals with be open to everyone to come to or if they will be mainly for Aboriginal people:

"No, that's for everyone," he says. "I was taught by my Uncle that if you're born here, you have the rights to learn the lore of this place. If you come here to live you still have the rights to learn, because, look at the first settlers, none of the mobs where the settlers came turned them away. They wanted to bring Cookie [Captain Cook] and Macquarie and all them fellas into the moiety systems. They had a place as a family group and they were going to be looked after; but like we know, they had their issues and they wanted the land for a different purpose. So even from the first settlers it was accepted for them to come into our systems and be part of it."

Clearly, the early settlers were ignorant of what was being offered to them. The cultural divide creating misunderstanding and fuelling prejudice. I wonder how things might have been different if they had been able to find curiosity, compassion and humility in encountering Aboriginal culture and how, perhaps, we can rectify those mistakes in some small way by attempting to arrive well today.

In Australia we have held National Sorry Day every year on 26th May since 1998 when Kevin Rudd as Prime Minister, made a formal apology from the government to the stolen generations for the countless atrocities of the Australian government in the past. Every year we say sorry for the wrongs done to the Aboriginal and Torres Strait Islander people, and it is a part of Reconciliation Week. Uncle Peter has brought me to tears at times by saying his own sorry to me and to all of us. He says as we sit in a café editing this chapter together:

"I'm sorry that since settlement, you've missed out on of our system and being a part of that.

I'm sorry that you missed out on being a part of our culture right from the beginning.

I'm sorry you missed out on our dancing, missed out on our stories.

I'm sorry that you missed out on singing Country and being a part of Country and lore."

I have to say it was quite a moving moment. This is what reconciliation is about. "It goes both ways," he says. Being truly sorry for the injustices, misunderstandings and losses of the past, we learn from each other in friendship, hoping that we can do better today. I ask if becoming a part of the moiety system is something non-Aboriginal people can seek out today, the way that those early settlers should have done at the beginning, though I'm concerned about asking about this when so much has been taken. I worry that I am not allowed to ask about it and I might be being inappropriate even after everything that Uncle Peter has said.

I have non-Aboriginal friends who have worked with

Aboriginal communities and as a result were given a moiety. I know the moiety system is complex and not one that will be adequately described in a few words. I urge you to look into it more from Aboriginal sources, but as simply as I can inadequately describe, it is a system where moiety names are given, usually depending on one's relationships within the family, though they can be assigned by a community if there is a need. From this, one has a responsibility to look after many different animals, plants, places, ceremonies and artforms, as well as to teach and share with others in the system.

The four animals of Kangaroo, Goanna, Echidna and Emu are the ones Uncle Peter spoke about from his Country. Moiety means 'half' in Latin referring to the complementary nature of the different groups. It is not an Aboriginal word, but it is commonly used to explain this system by Aboriginal people. The moiety gives a person identity within the group, as well as responsibilities, restrictions, and access to certain pathways of learning through the system of songlines and stories that relate to places and people. It is an integral part of the Aboriginal system of learning and relating to one another.

To be offered a moiety comes with responsibility. It is not to be confused with the new age concept of having a 'spirit animal,' though often there is also a spiritual element to it too. This would be an oversimplification and a cultural misrepresentation. I explain my hesitation, but also my interest and Uncle Peter explains that the knowledge is there to be learned:

"If people want to know from me, I can teach. I love to teach. So, when I go home for trips, which is nearly every school holiday, if people want to come and be part of the trip, part of the journey, just jump in your car and come along."

We continue to talk about his dreams of creating a centre of learning in Brewarrina that everyone can to come to. His idea is to have learning spaces, galleries and festivals there where everyone can come to learn about culture. It is inspiring. Uncle Peter is very open to sharing, and I am intrigued to learn more about it all. In the forefront of my mind, however, is the need for Aboriginal people's connection to culture to take a place of priority and I hope I can do my part in supporting that however I can in ways that are led by Aboriginal people. Non-Aboriginal people should not be 'taking' from Aboriginal culture. There has been enough taking. It is time to step back, but lean in. It is time for just listening, learning and accepting. If we learn enough to be invited in further through the moiety system, then we receive that with the respect it should have been given from the very start, understand the responsibility to the Earth that comes with it. When in Australia, we can learn more about Australian Indigenous cultures, and wherever we are in the world, we can make an effort to do right by the First Peoples of those lands, on their terms. Then, we all might come to hear that pulse of the land that Uncle Peter spoke of. It begins with arriving well today.

In This Together
with Bruce and Patricia Shillingsworth

I'm eating some pasta in a café in Broadway Shopping Centre. My son is beside me, absorbed in playing a video game, but still listening. We are there with Uncle Bruce Shillingsworth and his wife Patricia, or Aunty Trish who is from the Uralaroi nation. Uncle Bruce is explaining:

"One of the reasons why First Nations people are fighting for land, it's not just for the land, it's that everything that connects to the land connects to Mother Earth. It's the spirits that we deal with and it's our existence, it's identity.

"If we look at the beginning of time, since the first sunrise, *Biame* the Great Spirit, has given us our laws and the rules of how to live and how to live with each other and live with Mother Earth. So, what's it's done is give us our totem system. My totem is the Pedemelon or *Barnba* in Budjiti language, so I would never kill the Pedemelon or eat the Pedemelon. My sole responsibility is to protect it so that it doesn't become extinct. So right across the nations, right around the different nations, we all have our totems. We got an individual one, we got a group one, we got a clan one, we got a tribe or a nation totem. And that was to protect all the living creatures, right across this continent. Then none of the living creatures or species, even the plants would ever become extinct. That's how we survived for eighty plus thousands of years. We had a system in place that was given to us by the Great Creator since the beginning of time, so I think that's how we live sustainably with our environment.

"But, since early contact, a lot of our stuff has disappeared, because of the invasion, because of genocide, because of massacres, because of all those bad things that have happened in our history. So, what we're trying to do now, and I believe we're in a special time in history, is we're now starting to bring all those things back. We're learning, we're educating, we're bringing our language back, our stories, our dreaming, that were taken since colonisation.

"'So, what we need to do, I believe, with our children – and our children are our next generation, they're our next leaders – what we need to do is start teaching them, passing down our knowledge. Pass down the eighty plus thousand years of history, knowledge and wisdom down through to our next generation.'"

As he explains, Uncle Bruce is gesturing to Lugh, my son, and I ask if he means not just to the next generation of Aboriginal children... "Yes, not just First Nations, all children," he confirms:

"And that's why I work in schools now. I believe that we live in a multicultural society, and multicultural kids from all nationalities are going to teach the true history of this country. They're going to tell the true history. My history is their history, and their history is my history. We've got to embrace that. For so long, over the last two hundred and thirty plus years, we've been excluded, so now, I see a big movement with young activists, young leaders are now coming forth, they're bringing that to the forefront."

As we eat and drink among the hubbub of the busy café, we talk about environmental issues, the importance of the River systems and the trees, and how the totem system can be a part of all of our learning if we are sure to go about that learning with respect to protocols. Bruce talks about the importance of respecting local Indigenous cultures and the role of Elders as we learn more about it:

"What a lot of non-Indigenous people don't realise, they don't know the protocols which in First Nations culture is very important and they've got to respect that. They've got to really take a backwards step in a lot of the things that we do, like decision making.

"If I come here to Gadigal country, I've got to go through the process of talking to Gadigal people. I can't just go onto their land and do what I want. I just can't go onto their land and tell my story on their Country – I've got to get permission. Because it's their Country, it's their law/lore. It's their Dreaming, and we've got to respect that.

"So why we lived with approximately five hundred nations together is because we had that relationship, we had that respect in First Nations' culture, and I think we have to go back to that. Paying respect to the land where we are, and with the people, is important. And we give the Elders that respect, empowering them.

"And that's why we've been placed in that specific region, right across Australia, and what connects us is our stories, our songlines that connects us right across the nation, and once we start upsetting that, we break the balance. By speaking on someone else's land, by doing things on someone else's land, and it's the same with non-Indigenous people coming into our country and doing whatever they want. So, we're breaking the balance, the natural balance, and that's a cycle that the Great Creator put in place."

I realise there is so much for me to learn. For all of us to learn. I am only beginning to understand how this really functions. Though I'm learning more all the time, it can be difficult to work out how to do the right thing. I wonder about how I can integrate my own ancestrally inspired spirituality. I ask about how we can simultaneously respect local Indigenous culture and pay respects to our own ancestral traditions.

Uncle Bruce says:

"What I think we've got to do is go back and learn all that stuff. We got to learn it so we know. It's about truth telling as well. And it goes back to your role where you sit. What I see, especially through the spirit, moving across the Earth now, moving across our planet, a lot of First Nations people are now rising, and they're now coming back with their knowledge, their wisdom, and the spirit to guide them, and I think it's so important today that we do that. I think we've got the answers for the problem in our world today – we've got to look back at the ancient cultures, the things that we've been doing for thousands of years, to be able to solve the problems that have been happening – especially with climate change, global warming, social problems in our communities – we've got to go back to that."

Aunty Trish has been showing her agreement as Uncle Bruce explains and adds "Every non-Indigenous person should have an Indigenous friend. That way they can build that relationship. They'll know their boundaries."

We talk about how this is not something that just happens at a government level, it is a ground level shift where our personal relations and friendships play an important role in creating change. I am incredibly grateful to be sitting there with them sharing a conversation over a meal. We discuss values, decolonisation and the role of capitalism and commodification have had within colonisation as a destructive force. I ask Uncle Bruce to explain his take on what decolonisation means. He explains:

"The land and everything has to be given back to First Nations, the practices have to stay alive, the way they do things needs to be supported by non-Indigenous people, and I think we've got to decolonise our minds in the way we think and how we treat each other. We've got to take away the colonial way of doing things. The oppressive way of doing things. The coloniser, they oppressed us for so many years, so we've got to change some of their policies, some of their laws and the ways they've done things so it doesn't continue in the future, like the stolen generation. And it happens through a better understanding of Aboriginal culture and working together.

"Reconciliation is coming together, sharing our stories, telling the truth, changing the future so those sad things don't happen in the future again. I think it's about bringing back the language, bringing back our culture, bringing back our traditions, and then living and being supported in the modern world."

We talk about the importance of education in both systems and the importance of learning through oral culture for all of us. We talk about the land and how it holds knowledge within the Aboriginal system. We talk about getting kids out of classrooms and into the world, not only to experience the depth of wisdom that oral culture has to teach us, but also the importance it has for our understanding of sustainability and looking after the Earth. Uncle Bruce explains:

"You've got to be connected to the land. When you get out there you got to walk and you've got to talk to the land, talk to the trees, talk to the animals, you've got to feel that. You won't get it in the school or in the classroom with four walls. We look at nature, we look at the animals, the birds and the trees, all that. That all has a meaning to us. They're living things and they're part of our survival. Then you've got a very close connection, to the environment, and to Mother Earth."

We ponder how far the songlines might have travelled and talk about possibilities of them reaching distant parts of the world and their ancient cultures. We talk about the times when the sea levels were lower and the possibility of the people travelling with their stories across the lands there and to other continents, and we ponder the possibilities of reawakening those connections across the world today. Every place filled with Indigenous story, with each place having people pay respect to the Indigenous Elders there. It's a beautiful vision for how the world may have been and how it could be again.

I ask them about the Yaama Ngunna Baaka tour and how that came about. That's where I met them and it's an important part of their work in bringing all parts of our communities together to learn and share. They told me about the terrible state of the river and that:

"The only way we could think of was to go back to our traditional way, healing and singing the land. While our government and non-Indigenous people are just destroying it, and they're doing it the way that they want to do it. I said 'we've got to have a corroboree; we've got to get back to the old way our old people have done it.

"And what we did, we formed a group on a convoy and we brought the dance back, bringing the people together. The nations' dances together and they come back on their traditional land. I think it's about respecting and singing the spirits, talking to the spirits, talking to the land, talking to the river which is so important. I wanted non-Indigenous people to come on board, to be a part of that and to experience it and to be able to solve all the issues in our community, talk about it. I believe that non-Indigenous people need to be healed in this country, and First Nations people need to be healed, but the only way we're going to do it is to come together and heal together and that's what Yaama Ngunna Baaka is all about.

"I think it's a once in a lifetime opportunity for people who went out there. They had a great time and they've learnt a lot, and it's bringing the two cultures together. It's also reviving our culture, the rainmaker dance, bringing all that back, teaching our kids, passing it on, getting our Elders involved, talking about those old stories, building friendship, all that."

We finished our lunch and said goodbye, making some plans to learn more together and hopefully to head out to the next trip to the Rivers soon. There is a deep shared love of the Earth, of our ancestors and of the traditions we are a part of. We come together as friends and learn about what each other care about, how to be kind to each other, how to support each other, and how to be in the land and on Country with respect wherever we are and whoever we are. We are in this together.

The Elder Trees

...what if I am not only human, but also part of the mountain,
and the mountain is part of me? – Doug Ezzy

"It's OK, I'm going to head down this way," I say, as my friend and
I decide to part ways for a while as we wander the forest trails in the
Bunya Mountains. He decides to stay here and I take the path along
the creek. We had just been sitting with an enormous strangler fig tree
that had long since taken the place of the tree it first began winding
its tendrils around decades before. I nestled in the branches and my
friend took a photo. We were quiet, but we were taking a moment to
think about the meaning of that tree's journey. Later, he would tell
me of how it spoke to him of death and rebirth, and that he would see
past the ruthlessness of its name, implying it takes the life of the tree
that hosts it, instead it would speak of how the plants work together to
create a community of mutual support of one another – the larger tree
that was once there, supporting the young vine, would later die, yet the
vine would continue to support the community of plants and insects
that relied on the tree before. Things are not always what they seem.

The forest speaks of complexity and we find our own places to sit
and listen more deeply...

As I walked, I noticed the ground was covered in leaf litter and
was bone dry. The air was hot. As I had driven up here from the Blue
Mountains, the land was parched. Lithgow to Mudgee, Coonabarabran
and Moree, all dusty dry, struggling in severe drought, and the
mountains, strewn with soaring Bunya nut trees, were just the same,
though this was not normal at all. There was concern for the rainforest.
The creeks should be flowing. The floor should be damp and full of leaf
mould to nurture the plants of the forest floor, but it was all bone dry.

I meandered down the path by the creek bed, looking for a space to
sit for a while and listen. I wandered until I found a rocky corner where
a little moss grew over the rocks in the shade. The grey stone boulders

gathered around a drop off of a few meters which, in rainy times, must have been a waterfall. I sat and wondered about the loss of the water and looked around me. The moss seemed rare and precious. Some of the trees were quite large, but there was a sense here, as in many other places I had been, that these trees could be much bigger and that the largest of them had probably been removed for logging.

I sat quietly and didn't so much 'wait', but just 'was' in the place. I listened to the wind. I looked at the way the stones had fallen. I looked at the trees around me...

"There were huge ancient trees here once. Our mothers," they said. I could see them, towering over the others, making the forest that remained today look like saplings.

"They took care of us," they said, and I saw the huge root systems of the elder trees under the earth, reaching out in care and kindness to the smaller trees around them, bringing moisture up from the depths.

"They were our wisdom keepers; our Elders. They provided for us in life, and when they fell to the Earth, they would continue their care as they provided food with their bodies," they said, and I saw the mycelium networks converting the wood of fallen trees into food for growing plants, the soil being nurtured by the dead wood, the abundance of seeds planted as the large tree fell, and the heart wrenching emotional loss of a parent being taken away from their children as the loggers came.

A forest without its Elders; a forest of orphaned children struggling to survive without the knowledge of being that the Elders held; the wisdom of ages and knowledge of fires, floods and droughts, crafted into their limbs – lost and forgotten; knowledge not passed on; a generation of the passing on of tree wisdom, stolen. How will we know how to adapt, survive and change without them?

"We still grow, but we grow without our mothers who held us in their protection," they say, and I can see the roots like arms and hands, mothers holding children, being torn apart.

"They caught the clouds and brought the rain. Their roots dug deep into the earth to find water that we couldn't reach. They fed us and *looked after us. We needed them, and now they are gone."*

"We have lost the ancestors of our forest," they say, and I feel the heartbreak and loss.

"Don't forget your own ancestors," they say. "Remember. Reach back to the past and plan for a distant future."

Later, I return to the group and speak for these ancient trees and their lost children in a ritual we held. Others spoke for the animals of the forest, the birds harmed by fire, the rivers parched and dry, and the strangler fig, so misunderstood...

We Belong to the Earth

What is it to truly belong to a place? Of course, those who are Indigenous to the place they live in as First Peoples have an unquestionable connection to the land. Their belonging is unshakable, despite the struggles they have often faced in maintaining that grasp due to imperialistic colonising forces. But what of those of us displaced from the lands of our Indigenous ancestors? How do we belong to the land when we are new to a place? How do we move into right relationship with place, and with the communities that already belong there when we live in a world of colonial and environmental injustices? What is it that crafts true belonging? And how can we respectfully foster that within ourselves?

In the previous chapter, I am recalling my experiences at a gathering called a Council of All Beings. These gatherings are described as opportunities for rituals of mourning, remembering, and speaking from the perspective of other life-forms, particularly those of the wild natural world who cannot speak for themselves. In the gatherings, participants are encouraged to share their worries and troubles in regard to environmental concerns and their connections to the natural world; their sadness, loss and grief over the destruction of wild places that are deeply loved. Individuals take time to listen and observe in nature, particularly paying attention to messages presented by the natural world about its needs. The participants later meet in a ritual of council, taking on the personas of the parts of nature they connected with, and speaking needs from their perceived perspective.

The process is moving, and ultimately shifts our consciousness away from individualism towards collective identity with the natural world, helping us to see how integral those connections are. At its best, the experience is cathartic, healing and deeply insightful for all those involved, not only providing a space for personal healing, but also bringing greater enthusiasm and motivation for participants to fight for the rights of the land that they feel not only responsible for, but feel a part of.

John Seed, an environmental activist and eco-ritualist, explains this in the 2007 book *Thinking Like a Mountain: Towards a Council of All Beings*. He discusses a time when he was protesting the destruction of a rainforest in New South Wales, Australia. He says:

"There and then [at the protest] I was gripped with an intense, profound realisation of the depth of the bonds that connect us to the Earth, how deep are our feelings for these connections. I knew then that I was no longer acting on behalf of myself or my human ideas, but on behalf of the Earth... on behalf of my larger self, that I was literally part of the rainforest defending itself."

This turn away from individualistic thinking of 'I, me, my mine' towards the collective needs of 'we, us, our and ours', relating that to the whole of the Earth, including the non-human natural world, stands in stark contrast to the profit-focused, capitalistic, imperialism of corporate interests that promote greed, commodification, environmental destruction and cultural insensitivity. Even as corporations remove themselves from individual persons, having agendas as entities in themselves, they are unable to exist in an integrated way with the world around them.

Humans have a capacity to be in the world and to be a part of the Earth community that corporations do not. Corporations, despite their name containing the Latin word *corpus* meaning 'body', do not have bodies. They do not have senses of sight, hearing, touch, smell or taste with which to interact with the world as a being. In the Irish tale of Cormac and his journey to the land of Tír na nÓg, the sea God Manannán shows Cormac the

Fountain of Knowledge. The fountain has five steams flowing from it which are explained to be the five senses; no one can have knowledge who does not drink from the five streams and from the fountain itself. The teaching in this beautiful old tale of the Indigenous ancestors of Ireland, shows the importance of sensing the natural world to find wisdom.

Looking to the traditions of my ancestors that inspire me, many of the Celtic wisdom traditions look to the senses in nature and to the expansion of consciousness into an awareness of other life-forms that comes with these moments of contemplation. The poetry of the medieval Welsh poet Taliesin shows a wonderful example of this. The lengthy poem in the *Book of Taliesin* named 'A Hostile Confederacy' includes many lines explaining the poet's knowledge of the natural world gleaned, not only by their observations, but also, clearly, by either an extension of consciousness or perhaps a memory of past lives in other forms. Nevertheless, the poet explores the possibility of understanding what it is like to be able to speak from the perspective of other life-forms. In one part of the poem, he explores the nature of water as it relates to *Awen*, a word that literally means 'sacred breath' and is associated with the inspiration of poets, and a spiritually powerful force of creation, creativity and knowing:

The Awen I sing,
From the deep I bring it,
A river while it flows,
I know its extent;
I know when it disappears;
I know when it fills;
I know when it overflows;
I know when it shrinks;
I know what base
There is beneath the sea.

Through the power of inspiration, the poet knows the unknowable. Similarly, in the poetry of the Irish poet Amergín who, as chief bard to the Sons of Míl in the stories of the *Lebor Gabála Érenn*, shows the importance of knowing the land, as he steps ashore for the first time, exclaiming his song which begins:

> *I am the wind upon the ocean*
> *I am a wave upon the sea*
> *I am the murmur of billows*
> *I am an ox of seven fights*
> *I am an eagle upon a rock*
> *I am a ray of the sun...*

And later, when speaking a poem to calm a torrent of wind and storm caused by the Druids of the Tuatha Dé Dannan, that threatened to sink their ships, he called out:

> *Surging is the fruitful sea*
> *Fruitful are the hills planted out in rows*
> *Planted out in rows like the rainy woods*
> *Rain that flows to the river of waterfalls*
> *Waterfalls that fill the lake of pools*
> *Pools that fill the well on the hill...*

Showing here that his understanding of the beauty of the land, and his expression of that in poetic art, could bring peace and calm waves on the ocean's surface. These ancestral poets understood the importance of listening to the land, and that our belonging to place was bound up with our ability, not only to listen and observe, but to sing out that understanding as a form of magic that brought peace.

Our own belonging to place requires these things from us. We can't belong if we are not willing to listen, to engage, to really hear, and to see ourselves as a part of something bigger than an individual trapped by the whims of corporate demands. And we don't belong because we choose to. We belong when we become accepted by what we hope to belong to. We are the Earth. She welcomes us to her. We all belong to the Earth, together, and when we take time to listen, she speaks.

The Land Speaks
with Kristoffer Hughes

I recently met on Zoom with Kristoffer Hughes of the Anglesey Druid Order in Wales to record a podcast. As a native person of Wales and Indigenous to that place, he spoke of his connection to the land in a way that was so resonant of what Uncle Bruce, Aunty Trish and Uncle Peter had said. We wondered at the connections between all indigenous cultures of the world through story and song. Of course, clearly, there are large cultural differences, however, there is something about the human experience in connection with the Earth that brings all Indigenous traditions of the world together somehow.

We began the conversation talking about his upcoming trip to Bala to meet with fellow organisers of his Druid order and how special that place is to him. It is the setting of the story of Taliesin and Cerridwen, a tale of great importance to modern Druidry, of a boy who discovers the sacred inspiration of *Awen*, and is chased on a shapeshifting adventure through land, sea and sky, by Cerridwen the Goddess of inspiration, to be reborn as the greatest bard of all Britain. I ask him to describe why a visit Bala will be so special for him. He explains:

"Bala is the legendary home of Cerridwen and her family. That is where her legend arose. It is where her legend was located within the Welsh Bardic tradition, and within local lore and mythology. And whilst I live maybe an hour and a quarter away from Bala, here on the Island of Anglesey, and I get a sense of Cerridwen wherever I am – that power of Awen and inspiration – there's nothing quite like being in a place that has the very seat of a myth. That really does something to you somehow.

"I remember I was talking to Damh the Bard about it when we were flying over to Australia two years ago, and he was saying the same thing, that it doesn't matter where he is in the world, he has a sense the Awen is flowing, but nothing beats being in that particular location. So, it always feels a bit of a pilgrimage, being able to go to these places. I feel very fortunate that we live within a kind of mythological landscape as well as a sacred landscape. I've never taken that for granted."

We talk about the formation of the Anglesey Druid Order as a rekindled seat of learning, inspired by stories of it being one in the times of the Roman occupation in Britain. He explains how important connection to place is to the order's purpose:

"We just wanted, or primarily I wanted, a place where people could fall in love with the place [Anglesey] on a spiritual level as well as on a physical level because it's a beautiful place but spiritually, this island has a particular essence; a particular quiddity to her nature that is intriguing and enchanting, and I love that people, not only fall in love with the place but they fall in love with each other. I love that Druidry connects people and it connects people to place. So, at that very foundational level of my connection to the order, that's what sings to my spirit – it's that profound connection of people with place, and place with people, and all of the other inhabitants of kin that occupy this space – the seen and unseen."

Our conversation meanders through topics of language, cultural appropriation, colonial disruption of culture in Wales, and the ways that myths travel and change, but still come back to place. We talk about the idea of songlines in Aboriginal culture here in Australia and Kristoffer muses on the similarities of that idea of a song of the land within Welsh culture and the Bardic tradition:

"The Bardic tradition, whilst to a non-Welsh hearing ear,

they're hearing poetry being recited, but within the Welsh language, the poetry is being referred to as a *cân* which is a song, but it's a song that you don't necessarily learn, as such, but more of a song that you discover; that you find... I'm reluctant to use the word 'channel' because it's a loaded word, but it's more of a song that you find within the landscape and within relationship, and that the song somehow reflects not only the conversation that you're having with the land, but also how that conversation may inspire other people to connect to their own landscape.

"There's so much of that in the Welsh Bardic tradition, and so much about preserving things that were culturally significant by means of songs. And whilst yes, it's not a song in the traditional English-speaking sense of something that is rhythmic and lyrical and has music, but the metering is so strict and so profoundly complicated that it does create alliteration – it creates a melody by the sound of the voice.

"What I love about the Welsh tradition is the belief within the Bardic tradition that every single word has an animistic principle and that every time you speak, you speak with the voices of the dead, that those words have been used before, that they have a resonant alliteration, a quality that connects you to everyone who's ever used that word, and I love that. I love that language is animated; that language is a stream; an eternal river that carries all of these songs and that we might sing different lyrics to those songs, but that the tune or the melody is always the same and that we bring different lyrics. And then, of course, when our experience in this world ends, the lyrics stop and we just fall back into the song; into that original song, and then we become a part of that originality; of that origin."

We wonder at the beauty of the similarities and differences of these cultures across the planet; the ways they speak of the human experience and how that is reflected in different ways by the lands in which they were created. We discuss how stories shift and change as they move across lands or find themselves in different locations, but still hold a deep connection to the places where they were created. The diversity somehow reflecting the orchestra of song in which each of us plays a part in the great song of the Earth.

Rituals of the Earth

Rituals are a public affirmation of meaning, value, connection.
They tie people to each other, to their ancestors and to their
place in the world together. – David Suzuki

As I write, I hear the mumblings of a news report my husband
is watching in the other room. He is at home today because of
flooding danger. There has been heavy rain along the eastern
coast of Australia for the last few days and severe floods have
torn homes into the rivers, damaged countless properties,
closed roads and schools and businesses, and left communities
stranded in evacuation centers. We are lucky this time, to be
living on the top of a mountain rather than in the plains, but
during the bushfires, the dice roll of chance meant we were the
ones in danger.

In times of extremes, there is an urge in us for vigil; for
acknowledgement of the forces around us that threaten and
challenge us, and inevitably cause grief as we tally the losses
and look ahead to the possibilities of recovery.

I can't quite imagine what it is like to be flooded. I have never
lived in a place that was threatened in that way, but I do know
what it is like to have enormous bushfires on two sides of the
small town I live in, with it burning just a couple of kilometres
away. In the summer of 2019-2020 the fires here burned 20 million
hectares across Australia with 5.5 million of those in NSW where
I live. Our home is in the middle of an enormous national park
on both sides of the town, so we were not able to leave, but had
to commit to staying and trying to look after it. As the wall of fire
got closer, I watched the coverage on the news, but I also saw
it in the videos made by friends living in neighbouring towns
as they took a moment to film the red-hot ashes falling on their
backyards as the fires blazed across the street from them while

they ran for the garden hose to put out the spot fires on the lawn. It was all so close to home. The need to do something, anything, in the face of this felt urgent. Of course, the first thing we did was prepare ourselves with the practical work. We made sure our home had enough hoses and buckets available. We trimmed overhanging branches and got rid of leaf litter in the gutters and under the trees. We made sure friends knew they could come to us if they needed to leave. We found out where the local evacuation centres and safe meeting places were. But this was done in a few days, and the fires burned for months. Life just went on, and of course there were times when we cried for all the losses and sat and wondered what more could be done.

I realised at this time that there was a need, not only in my local community, but in the global community who also had their eyes on us and our burning land. Friends in the UK and USA were asking how they could do a ritual for us. They wondered what weather pattern would bring the rain so that they could envision that pattern. They wanted to know if it was appropriate to call on Aboriginal gods and goddesses to bring the rain, or if there were special prayers that could be said. I knew there was something I could do, so I wrote a ritual for the fires.

The ritual worked on several levels. We did not call on Aboriginal gods and goddesses as this would not be appropriate unless we had the direct guidance of an Aboriginal Elder. Instead, we acknowledged the Traditional Custodians of the land we stood on, the Elders past and present, and the deep and abiding connection First Nations have to the land as I have described in previous chapters. This recognition is poignant in a ritual where we acknowledge that the land is burning out of control due to a neglect of understanding of traditional land management practices. We then focused the ritual on the balancing of elemental energies, asking that the winds blow moisture from the ocean to the land bringing rain; that the fires are acknowledged and calmed, and that we find the fire we need within ourselves to fight for renewed peace; that the waters of life flow from the skies and into the earth and waterways; that the earth would be quenched and restored, healed and renewed.

In Australia, fires are not always destructive. Cultural burns are controlled and work to clear underbrush, encourage grassland for grazing animals like Kangaroos and Emus, and regenerate seeds of plants that have evolved to benefit from burning. Fire itself is not bad. Fire is an integral part of the balance of life in the Australian landscape. It can, however, become out of balance and when not adequately managed, can become dangerous and destructive.

Acknowledging the importance of Indigenous connections to land, the imbalance that has been created as a result of neglect and mismanagement in the present, that is, a need for a rebalancing in nature and in the elements that make up the world around us can be an important part of our rituals and help us all to become better custodians of the lands in which we live. Trebbe Johnson writes about the power of ritual to help us to deal with the atrocities of environmental damage in the world, whether it is damage caused by humans or by natural disasters. In her 2018 book *Radical Joy for Hard Times,* Johnson explores how creating beauty in damaged places can bring healing to us all, and the urgency to learn how to do so increases for us all as we experience a world with disasters becoming a part of life more and more frequently. Fire, flood, drought, and sandstorms have become a part of everyday life here where I live in the last few years. The world is changing and weather events are becoming more extreme. As such, this is work that we will all need to face in one way or another as time goes by.

Johnson outlines rituals she calls an "Earth Exchange" where participants visit a wounded place to sit with it, share stories of what the place means to them, sharing their emotional connections with it, and then creating beauty and art together there as a gift for the healing of the place. Johnson gives examples that are both natural and caused by human neglect. In this way we could consider any loss to the natural and human world. Natural occurrences – not just those caused by climate change, but also those caused by nature's extremes – such as fire, flood, drought, hurricanes and cyclones, tsunamis, volcanic eruptions, sandstorms – can be considered, as well as occurrences more directly linked to human neglect: pollution, mismanagement, abandonment and overdevelopment. Any loss of the natural world that causes grief can be acknowledged in this way, and our rituals and spiritual observances are one way that we can give back beauty and art as a gift for these broken places, for their healing and for our own. Johnson explains:

"The practice of giving a gift of beauty to a wounded place subtly, yet fundamentally, changes my relationship with the place. How could such a seemingly simple act make such a difference? For one thing, I have tested the mettle of my own courage and found it to be strong. I have dared to touch the monster. I have realised that not only am I not dragged down into some loathsome circumstance from which I cannot escape, but that just the reverse occurs: I see the place transform, like a character in a fairy tale, from a deficient and debilitated thing to a presence that impels an expression of love that I myself am uniquely qualified to give."

Ritual and art are healing. They are acts of recognising all the components that make up the present moment: the place we stand in; what the world is made up of; our own connections as individuals and as a group; the time and space that we are moving through in this place; and how our connection with this place in the moment is shaping us. Ritual is a practice of bringing in and recognising all that is in the present moment: honouring it; feeling it with all our emotions and expressing that connection through the beauty of art in some way. The art could include sharing heartfelt stories and tears, placing a leaf or stone with reverence as a gift, singing a song, making music, sharing poetry or dancing. Simple gifts that leave no trace leave an energetic shift, a memory in the fabric of space and time, that will be felt in times to come.

Ritual offers us an opportunity to sit with the land as it is, and be who we are in the moment, shaped by the forces of nature and circumstance around us. We grieve with the land, and we hope with her and heal with her. We are nor separate from nature. We are a part of the environment as much as the Earth herself is a part of us. But ritual is not only about healing and grieving. Ritual itself can be a key to learning, wisdom and understanding, and to the Earth-based traditions of the world.

The Earth Gorsedd

We decided to gather in a lovely wide-open space in a city park in Adelaide. It was easy for everyone to get to. There were about ten of us. The grass in the park was a vivid green from being tended, but the bushland around it was very dry, just like the hundreds of kilometres of dry bushland I'd travelled through in the week before. The green was beautiful but it felt unnatural, and the comfort that came with it, shallow. I had just finished my trip to the rivers and came with a heavy heart. We had planned the gathering before my trip through our shared concerns as Druids about the sad state of the environment. At the time the fish kills in the rivers and lakes were on our minds, as well as the burning of the Amazon (our own devastating fires were yet to come), and the lack of action on climate change.

We had come together to share a gorsedd ritual. A gorsedd is a Welsh world meaning a gathering of Bards for the purpose of an eisteddfod. Bards are storytellers, poets, song keepers and historians and when they share their work it is called an eisteddfod. A gorsedd is the ritual in which the eisteddfod occurs.

We named the gathering an 'Earth Gorsedd' because we had decided to come together to share stories, songs and poetry about the environmental destruction we had seen, our grief for it, and our hopes for change. We began by Acknowledging Country, calling for peace, calling in the elements to the directions, and honouring the ancestors of our bloodlines, traditions and the land. Then we spoke of the destruction we had seen – the hurt and harm and how we grieved for the earth. Each person was given time to share what was of concern to them, sharing how wide our concerns were over the Earth. We then took time to wander the garden, finding symbols of hope, messages from the Earth in tiny seeds.

I walked around, looking for something that seemed to speak to me. That green grass, so soft under my feet, was in such contrast to the dry riverbeds I had seen only days before. I bent and picked a few blades.

We returned to the circle and shared what the earth had spoken to us, laying them on our makeshift altar in the centre of the circle – a green cloth holding symbols of Land, Sea and Sky: a rock from the desert representing the Land; a bowl of water with a Celtic triple knot design representing the Seas and sacred waterways; feathers from an emu that was roasted for us at the river trip at Brewarrina representing Sky, air and spirit. There was also a beautiful bowl with emu designs by an artist in Wilcannia who gave me permission to use it in this ritual, paper daisy flowers, a big piece of river red gum bark, and other items that the group had brought along to represent their personal connections to the land. We added what we had found in our meditation...

A seed pod; a symbol of hope for the future. It takes time for change to happen. We need to be patient and let it grow.

A snail shell reminding us that sometimes it is ok to seek protection and move within – that our centre is soft and we can have a hard shell – to be kind to ourselves.

A stone, reminding us to stay grounded and strong. The Earth is so solid beneath us. She will be here, no matter what. Be here and now and do the best we can.

I laid down my blades of grass, so green and comforting here, but in a world of drought - a false comfort. A reminder not only that we should look further – outside of what we take for granted and what comforts us, because where we place our attention – where we feed the Earth, the Earth thrives.

We sang Awen together and then shared songs, stories and poetry. Some were by artists we loved, some we had written ourselves and, at the end, anyone could take a moment to speak from the heart about the change they hoped to see in the world.

We cried. It was healing. By the end of the ritual our sorrow had shifted into solidarity, with each other, and with the Earth that we love.

The Dam and The Gully
with David King

Eel looks you in the eye
Through gold rippling water
Asking,
What do you call this?
This concrete temple you built here,
What life does it serve
to celebrate?
Sarah Daniel

The Burragorang Valley isn't called that enough. Most people call that place 'the Warragamba Dam catchment area'. But once you know, you know, and then the Warragamba Dam seems like something that doesn't belong in a place that was brutally stolen. From then on, you'll call it the Burragorang Valley.

The dam wall was built between 1948 and 1960, so well within living memory, and the Aboriginal people living here still mourn its loss. With the inundation they lost a lot of important sites for their community and for their learning through songlines and dreaming stories. The government is looking at raising the dam wall further, and the Gundungurra people are fighting against it, along with many environmentalists and other concerned members of the community.

I had a chat over the phone with David King, a Gundungurra man here in Katoomba. He told me how the dam also sits on the major part of the course of the Gundungurra dreamtime story of Gurangatch the eel and Mirrigang the tiger quoll as they created the landscape and river systems. The songline starts in the Burragorang where the dam currently is, and moves up the river to Wombeyan, Jenolan and back up to Katoomba. If the dam wall is raised, access to additional sites on this important songline would be lost. He explained that this would be a major loss to the community if the dam wall is raised.

Around the time that the Burragorang Valley was flooded for the dam, many of the Gundungurra community made their way to stay at a place here in Katoomba called 'The Gully' or *Garguree* in Gundungurra language. Fortunately, it was not a strictly monitored mission or reserve as other communities had been forced into, so there were still some opportunities to share cultural knowledge. David explains how important it was to be in that place, but also how heartbreaking it is when Aboriginal people don't have access to the lands of their Dreaming stories and songlines:

"A lot of Aboriginal land across Australia is privately owned so you don't get that chance to function, so you feel like you're letting your Elders down. If you can't keep your moiety totem, skin process going then, technically, you haven't fulfilled what you're supposed to do.

"It's about ceremony, caring for country, keeping country alive, keeping your next generation's stories going so that there's that continual circle going, that continuing connection, without that access, so I've technically never journeyed on my Burrogorang clan country for ceremony like on my Mum's country in Gedumba clan. In Gedumba clan country I've been able to have that opportunity,"

He explains that he has been able to access two of his clan country areas and the ceremonial journeys associated with them, but not the third which is in the Burragorang Valley because it's a schedule one protected water area:

"It saddens me, because my maternal connection is through the Burragorang and thankfully I had a lot of uncles who talked to me when I was a kid who shared me the stories, but it's weird when you don't visualise it and walk on it, because walking country is a big thing. Getting access to Country – a lot of the difficulties and issues facing our culture is that no access or no right to practice your culture. You've been denied something that's a part of you and therefore you wonder why you break at certain points – you don't have that sense of peace and that sense of accomplishment."

He explains that the ecological impact of the dam wall being raised is also of concern to the Gundungurra community:

"Ecologically, the amount of trees and threatened species and flora and fauna that you would lose, you may never get back. There has to come a point where you just realise this Earth runs on a balance, and if you don't keep the balance then you see some of the decimation you see now. You just can't keep on spreading suburbs out for eternity, because you're in a finite place, it's not infinite.

"So apart from the cultural impacts and the environmental impacts, there's also the concept that we've got to start looking at the way we can be more responsible with our resource management. From an Aboriginal perspective, your resources were managed to continue, not to run out, there was no tipping point, there was no end of cycle, you always were confident your resources would be there and increasing, it's just a whole different world viewpoint. And I think the current viewpoint that's currently being utilised, compared to what was there for thousands of years."

The Gully has become an important place for the community to learn about this, as well as a significant place for the Gundungurra community. But they had to fight hard for this too. After settling there voluntarily as a result of the inundation, the community was uprooted to make way for the development of a racetrack in 1957. Thankfully, it was given back to the Aboriginal community after many years of fighting for it in 2002. The place is now a registered Aboriginal Place that is open to the public. Locals come together there to work on swamp care projects and to learn about caring for the land, and the history and culture of the Gundungurra community. David says:

"I do swamp care because it brings back Country, it brings back pathways, the plants and animals get a chance to come back home as well, and then the Aboriginal people that were connected to that site and that pathway can sit and dream again."

The old race track is being left to be reclaimed by nature a little more each day. The tarmac is being grown over by moss and grass. The metal railings are rusting. The wood is being reclaimed by fungus. The cover of this book is an artwork I painted myself of the leaf of a plant growing over the racetrack railings and road, showing the power of Mother Earth, or *'Gunai Dhaura'* in Gundungurra language, to restore the balance and reclaim the land as her own. David sees it that way too:

"We're just really thankful that *Gunai Dhaura* is bringing back her little home. It's beautiful. It's just great to see those little pathways starting to come through which were there for thousands of years, while it's cracking bitumen."

Other local artists have also felt moved to respond to these issues through art. A group of poets here collated their work for the 2019 book called *Listening to the Land: A poetic action against the raising of the Warragamba Dam wall*. In it, their poetry speaks of the needs of nature in the valley, and the concerns for the Aboriginal custodians of the land and others in the community in their attempts to save it from development, and if this is unachievable, to at the very least mourn the losses it threatens to bring. At the beginning of this chapter is a few lines from 'Eel Speaks' by Sarah Daniels, delving into the experience of the eel that finds itself trapped by the dam wall and wondering at its existence. As I read it, I imagine the ancestral memory of eels there telling them the way, but leaving them confused as the way is blocked. I wonder at the effect of our heavy handedness on the forms of the Earth.

In the introduction to the book, they ask us 'What do you hear when you listen deeply from your animal body, that place that still remembers intimately the threads of connection to, and entanglement with, the Earth to which it belongs?'. The poetic responses within the work engage with voices of 'Earth Kin' – the voices of nature that we are a part of. The poems speak of and from the perspectives of native animals, plants, stones, mountains and the dam itself. Extending their consciousness to explore how poetry can act as just as powerful a force as activism and protest, their words speak to the heart, and speak for those who cannot speak for themselves.

Much like the sentiments of those sitting in the Council of All Beings, these poets took time to listen to the land, and put themselves in positions to speak for the Earth itself, knowing that we are a part of the Earth. And through the process they asked, 'what is the link between poetry, community/civil society, environmental activism, and a reawakening of our emplaced connection to the living lands and Earth Kin that we fight for and with?'

Art and poetry tell stories, and through those stories, have the power to move hearts and minds. They speak of what is hard to express in explanations alone. They speak to the emotions and the spirit. It is in the heart that change begins. Art, in this way, can lead to positive change in the world, whether this is action against injustice, or acknowledging the need for grieving and healing. The injustices to the Aboriginal communities and the environment here are injustices to us all and we share that in our work as we fight for the changes we want to see, in activism, art and heartfelt community connections.

Layering the Wheel of the Year

I have written before about how we can adapt the traditional wheel of the year to our local environment in my 2017 book *Australian Druidry – Connecting with the Sacred Landscape* and I don't want to repeat myself too much here. In that book I gave a case study of the wheel of the year I created for where I was living at the time in the Northern Beaches of Sydney. Instead of just looking at the traditional wheel of the year and switching it by six months for our Southern Hemisphere seasons, trying to force celebrations from other lands onto this landscape, I tried looking at what was actually going on around me at those times of year and creating festivals and celebrations that were more relevant to my own environment.

To do this we do not need to let go of the old festivals entirely, as they have a relevance even outside of their original lands as stories of our ancestors and stories of agriculture, but we can question how to bring them into this place with sensitivity. Of course, learning how we can do so with respect to Indigenous cultures is of high importance, as is being present with what is actually around us, even as the world changes and shifts due to climate change and other influences in the environment.

As we explore our ancestral practices as the years turn, we can also become aware of layers of meaning that happen along with them. Some aspects of the traditional festivals feel entirely inappropriate in this land, often because of the specific nature of the festivals in context with their original environments. Others, however, remain relevant because they reflect something of our natural cycles of human activity that relate to seasonal change. To give some examples, we are often drawn to storytelling and crafts at midwinter; there is a sense of a balancing energy at the equinoxes as the days and nights become equal in length; the return of light in the spring brings inspiration and renewed creativity; and the height of light at the summer solstice representing the growth of vegetables and fruits in many orchards and gardens.

Importantly, as we explored the world around us, we noticed the patterns that we flow through each year and how they seem to represent something within ourselves and in our communities. Wattle blooms in abundance in many places from midwinter to spring and so can represent the return of the sun and the inspiration of spring. The barkfall of early summer represents letting go and clearing away what is not needed to make way for growth. The bushfires that threaten us every summer become symbols of rebirth, cleansing and regeneration. The storms of late summer represent fertility, the dance of life, childlike playfulness and joy. The relief that comes with the end of summer and storm season bring peace at the autumn equinox. The ancestors are acknowledged as we entered the darkest part of the year, with the symbol of the moon rising over the ocean.

Local Indigenous calendars also add layers to our understanding of these cycles. Their seasonal observations of when wildflowers bloom, or at what times migratory animals arrive and depart sit alongside our own personal observations. They also deepen them as we come to see how long these observations have been taking place and how the cycles of seasons change through time. There is so much to learn from Indigenous cultures in this respect when it is offered for us all to learn. The balance between these observations – ancestral, personal and Indigenous – is something we are all slowly and gently learning more about, as information is shared and relationships are built.

Since writing my last book, I have realised how this way of adding local observations to our practice can also help us to acknowledge and process the immediate urgency of environmental crises. Knowing it is midsummer and the traditional celebration is for abundance does not sit right when the garden is suffering due to drought and smoke from bushfires. Knowing a particular flower is blooming early and not 'on time' in relation to the symbols of the seasons in our wheel of the year, helps us to acknowledge changes in climate and other conditions. Our seasonal awareness and recognition of change becomes an integral part of our practice. It brings us into a sensitive awareness of the land around us. There is a necessity to observe what is happening in the moment and question what it means for us as a part of the place. Asking, 'how can this moment in all that is it, be recognised, acknowledged, and understood within our beings?' can help us not only to connect more deeply, but to heal ourselves and the places we are in.

I walked into the grove. It rang with familiarity. As I looked around the space, though I was alone, I could still remember who had stood around me the last few times we met here as a group. Around me were placed eight large pieces of sandstone, each marking a point on the compass, a direction out into the world, a season on the wheel, and elements of magic...

I remembered times I had met here with friends for rituals in the past. At Beltane we stood in a circle – about twelve of us. I walked the circle now, remembering, looking around. Just there, in the northern point, Ben had stood as he made a heartfelt Acknowledgement of Country as we all placed our hands on the Earth. In the west, Michelle had sat there as she shared a beautiful poem she had written, and in the north east Skye made up a story about the song of cicadas. I smiled. Good memories.

In the centre of the circle a large flat stone is close to the Earth. I remembered the sprinkling of rain and the lush green grass as we gave thanks for a year that had seen more rain than the last, ending the fires and bringing abundance to the land. We picked young fruits, flowers and herbs in the gardens and lay them on the centre stone, recognising the abundance that the rain brought. We made wishes that the summer to come, would continue to be kind. We shared our joy with the rain and our sadness for the losses of the year before.

Other rituals hung in the space too. The voices were different, the fruits changing to large apples, blackberries, potatoes, artichokes and nuts as the seasons moved on. Some days the rain brought water up to our ankles. Other days were sunny and warm, some cold and wintery.

Each one still sits vividly in my mind, as does the vision of the same place looking stark, dry and bare when the fires had raged across the distant valley... the air choking with smoke and the garden plants and trees wilting and losing leaves no matter how much we tried to water them with our little watering cans.

I sat in the circle alone, but I could hear the songs we sang in the circle when we were together, as though the stones around me remembered them and sang them back to me; the memories hung in the air there, waiting to be retrieved whenever we returned. The rituals made the experiences more vivid. The Earth remembered and so we would too.

As I looked around the circle, I saw not only stones marking a space, but marking: times in the year, sunset and sunrise, summer and winter, morning, noon and midnight. I saw celebrations and remembered friends' presence, words, voices and insights. The circle itself holding the memories of time, place and story...

Orality and Mnemonics

Orality is in our nature. People are storytellers and stories come alive most vividly when taken off the page and told in person. Speaking in this moment of the beauty of orality to you, through the written word seems bizarre. I wish you were here with me, to hear my voice and know how deeply these ideas move me from the way I express them to you. Words on a page are simply forms and shapes that recall memories within us of ideas. They don't tell the whole story. You only receive a part of my storytelling in the text – you are missing my tone of voice, the view out the window, the music I have playing in the background, the sun shining after a week of rain – it is possible for me to describe these things to you, but if we had been in the same space as I told this to you, it may well have stood in your memory more clearly – the story animated by the recall of context.

Our brains are well adapted to function with oral learning. Our memories work incredibly well when ideas are brought to us in certain forms that allow for fast recall. Stories, rhyming poems and song lyrics, dance and gesture can be learned and stay with us for years and years, even if left dormant for long periods of time. Have you ever heard an old song come on the radio and been surprised that you could remember all the lyrics? Or perhaps you remember the moves to a dance when you hear a particular tune? Sayings and turns of phrase, sometimes poetic, come to us in times of need, or tunes that help us to remember the alphabet or the colours in the rainbow. This is oral learning and it is powerful.

All over the world, people engage with a complexity of experience in story, song, music, dance art and ceremony to pass on knowledge, share understandings and seek wisdom. We do this every day as we live our lives: we tell stories of our days; we experience and remember the world around us in the context of place; and we share stories and memories of those experiences with others. It is a natural process to us, and for that reason it has stood the test of time as one of the greatest forms of knowledge keeping.

Indigenous cultures are often rich in oral culture. Storytelling about the land, and the role of the people within it, is integral to cultures that live in connection with their environments. In globalised, city-focused, industrialised societies there is also a presence of oral culture in advertising, movies and television, pop music, theatre and performance. However, the role of these has become less involved with the maintenance of knowledge and more focused on capitalism, entertainment and personal glorification of the performers. In contrast, Indigenous cultures make use of song, dance, poetry, music and performance for the maintenance of knowledge systems.

In Australian Aboriginal culture the terms 'Songlines' and 'the Dreaming' are often used to describe the complex systems of story, song, dance, ceremony, lore and law and how they relate to the landscape and to human connections. These are English words which have become popularised to explain the commonalities across Aboriginal culture of how the land connects to cultural practice and human relationships. There are many local Aboriginal language variations on this word such as the well-known *Tjukurpa* in Anangu, *Altjira* in Arrernte, and others, depending on the country they relate to. Here where I live it is *Nura* in Dharug language and *Gunyunggalung* in Gundungurra language. It is often referred to as a time long ago, or a creation time, but is also often expressed as occurring in the present moment, now and forever.

The whole system of stories, dances, songs and ceremonies relates to specific places in the landscape, and with those stories are held vast amounts of information about the land, its resources and the ways that people should relate to the land – to care for it, to maintain it, and to look after everyone and everything that is a part of it.

Margo Neale Ngawagurrawa, curator of the exhibition *Songlines: Tracking the Seven Sisters* explains in the accompanying book for the exhibition, that this "ancestral knowledge is fully integrated; it encompasses the disciplines that the Western world compartmentalises: medicine, law, astronomy, ethics." It is not separated into independent categories that we might be familiar with in Western learning, but instead brings these together in a complete and interdependent system of learning.

She also stresses that knowledge "disembodied and dislocated in books, photographs, and other media is unfathomable" to the Aboriginal people sharing their work in the exhibition; that the depth of complexity in a land-based oral knowledge system has its authority for them because it is "evidenced in the surrounding world". The exhibition explored how oral culture shares information in integrated ways with the landscape as what Neale calls the "master archive" holding the information.

Clearly, in Aboriginal culture the art of wholistic performance that included various elements of song, dance, knowledge and connection to place, is key to the maintenance of complex systems of knowledge, and not by any means used simply for entertainment – song, story, ceremony and dance held meaning that was not just important, but integral to survival, and to the sustainable management of people and the land and her people.

This does not mean the stories are without spiritual significance, of course. The integrated nature of the system means it is quite the opposite. Bruce Pascoe, author of the 2014 book *Dark Emu: Black Seeds: Agriculture or accident?* explains that:

"...there is no separation between the sacred and non-sacred as all actions are steeped in religious purpose. The mere act of burning grass has a specific story attached to it, a story that directs the need and benefits of the action in law."

Science, in this sense, is spiritual. The connection to the land integral to survival not only practically, but on a deeper level that had a scope for the whole function of society on a massive integrated scale. Pascoe goes on to explain that:

"...the songlines of Aboriginal and Torres Strait Islander people connected clans from one side of the country to another. The cultural, economic, genetic and artistic conduits of the songlines brought goods, art, news, ideas, technology and marriage partners to centres of exchange."

If we are to consider the innate ability of human beings for this kind of oral culture, it's conceivable to think that these webs of story, land, art and connection once spanned the globe, and in many ways still do, and it is the task of all of us to learn how to reconnect with the power of these cultures of orality, so that we might re-indigenise our ways of being and come into closer relationship with the land. Indeed, our survival may depend on it, and even more than that – our sense of spiritual connection, meaning and purpose in the world may do too.

I also believe that this way of understanding oral culture can help us to better understand the practices of our Celtic ancestors in Druidry. It offers a way of looking at story, song, landscape and the role of the bards that values them as a system of learning about the land and our care for it, as well as our care for each other. This is a window of understanding that is opening, and one that offers worlds of exploration for the curious learner.

Caesar commented of the ancient Druids that:

"They are said there to learn by heart a great number of verses; accordingly, some remain in the course of training twenty years. Nor do they regard it lawful to commit these to writing, though in almost all other matters, in their public and private transactions, they use Greek characters. That practice they seem to me to have adopted for two reasons; because they neither desire their doctrines to be divulged among the mass of the people, nor those who learn, to devote themselves the less to the efforts of memory, relying on writing; since it generally occurs to most men, that, in their dependence on writing, they relax their diligence in learning thoroughly, and their employment of the memory."

Often stories were told that related to specific places, landforms and landmarks, and to tell the stories in those locations would not only have awakened them to deeper meanings, but may also have presented opportunities to learn on a number of different levels, that could never be put down in writing because they are vast. So much may have been lost.

It's common to practice neo-Pagan Druidry in lands outside of the places where the original stories were created, telling the stories outside of their homelands. They speak of more than just the places they came from. But perhaps there is more to be discovered in exploring them as embodied within the land, and seeing that although we can take these stories with us in our hearts, they are always related to place, and the systems of story, song, dance and more can help us awaken the richness of what they have to teach us. Looking at both the stories of our ancestors, and the stories of the lands we are living in, respectfully, can be a part of this journey of learning more about the rich educational nature of embodied, oral learning.

Dancing the Earth
with Jo Clancy

"Flick your hands like this when you kick out your leg, like wings. You can put your head wherever you want. It's quite nice if we all look in different directions, see. Just be your own kind of lyrebird.

"Then we step fast for seven, then five, then three, with the last three like we are scratching the earth, but on the second time, we crouch on that last one and all say '*dyagula*' together,' Jo explained the steps of the dance.

"'OK. Let's go again."

Jo started singing the song in Wiradjuri language again as we moved across the polished hardwood floor of the stage area in the indoor amphitheatre at the local Steiner school, a masterfully hand built building of straw and mud walls, with tall windows draped with rainbow silk curtains and a backdrop through them of a sunset over the mountain bushland. The floorboards were cool under our feet, but we imagine dancing on the earth. A few minutes before we began dancing, Jo had explained that when she created the dance, while spending time on Wiradjuri Country that as she danced it over and over, creating the steps, the ground had become softer and dustier, so that by the end, as she flicked and kicked like a lyrebird building a nest, the dust flew in clouds. I could imagine it and saw it in my mind's eye as we danced in the hall.

"We might be able to do that one for the Winter Magic Festival if it's on," she tells us.

I was not able to make it to the last festival, so I really hope we can. Last year the local festival that brings everyone in the community to celebrate the magic of the mountains didn't happen at all because of the pandemic, but the year before I was filming a documentary about Paganism in Australia. I had really wanted to be a part of it though. We had learned a dance about bread, and we were going to wear beautiful Aboriginal art print costumes that said 'treaty' on the back of them. The reason for having the dance of bread was that Aboriginal people are probably the oldest living culture in the world to have a record of making bread from ground grains, and now, bread is eaten all over the world. It's something that we share.

When I ask Jo how she would describe what she does, she says that first and foremost, she is a mother, a daughter, a sister and an aunty and those roles and relationships shape everything that she does, but that as far as making a living goes, her life is dance. She explains that her work is multifaceted, not just teaching dance, but also "creating work" as she puts it, meaning making shows, educational programs and teaching in several different ways in both the Aboriginal community and the wider community.

Jo Clancy is an experienced Aboriginal teacher who works both as the Head of Cultural Practice with NAISDA (National Aboriginal Islander Skills Development Association) with their Dance College on the Central Coast, and here in the Blue Mountains. She founded and runs the Aboriginal women's dance group Wagana Dancers that performs dance through educational programs in schools and community gatherings, and teaches in the broader community, like the classes I get to attend.

I am sitting with Jo in the amphitheatre where we dance, recording a conversation about her work before class starts. I ask Jo whether it's important to her to share Aboriginal culture and dance with the wider community here as well as doing her traditional dance work:

"Yes. It is important to me, and I think one of the big reasons why that is important, is where we live. I've lived in the mountains for 42 years now. I've always lived off country. I'm a Wiradjuri woman, but I've never lived on Wiradjuri Country. I was born on Dharug Country in Sydney, and then

I've lived and raised my family on Dharug and Gundungurra Country, so I feel incredibly connected to this place, and it is the community of the mountains that is why I share dance the way that I do.

"It's such a beautiful community in the mountains. Lots of people want to engage with Aboriginal culture. They want to learn. They want to share with such genuine openness and respect and I don't think that's everywhere. I know that's not everywhere, I leave the mountains to work, so even though I don't live on my traditional Country, I spend a lot of time in Wiradjuri Country and have all my adult life. I've done a lot of dance development in the Central West. That's where I'm from; that's where my dance comes from and that's where I'm connected to. I have an obligation to work and share on Wiradjuri country, and in doing that, I know that there's many communities out west that don't have the same relationships with their non-Indigenous community that we do here in the mountains. So, I think that's a big reason why I do what I do here in the mountains."

We are certainly very lucky. I've felt incredibly moved by the opportunity to go to these classes. With each step I feel there is healing going on. Sometimes I've danced my pain or grief as I've been learning about the damage done to Aboriginal culture through history, the movements and Aboriginal language words in the songs pulling at my heart. I've also danced love and joy that these songs and dances are still with us, and still being created and shared. Often, through the movements, we dance connection and love for the Earth, our gestures speaking much more than we could describe with our words.

The movements we learn aren't only traditional Aboriginal dance, they also include contemporary Indigenous dance, as well as lots of balance, flexibility, strength and fitness training. In the contemporary dance, traditional Aboriginal elements are included and references to nature are very important: we point to stars; we move like emus or dingoes; we hold our arms in a circle to represent the moon; we flap our wings like dancing brolgas; we reach down and imagine we are gathering sand in our hands... Each step a reminder of the natural world, and an expression of our connection with it, and our love of it.

Jo tells me the story of how the *dyagula* (Lyrebird) dance was created:

"That was pretty special that one. I was on Country in Kandos fairly close to *Ganguddy* which is known as Dunn Swamp. I was on a residency with six other Aboriginal women. I was the only dancer – they were all visual artists. We were staying in this farmhouse and it was a bit, I don't know... farmhouse creepy?' she laughs.

"I wake up really early. So, I woke up the first day of the residency, it was really cold, so I thought, 'Alright, I'll layer up and I'll go walking,' and there was *dyagula*, which is our word for Lyrebird, in the scrub, and I was like, 'Oh that's cool, that's great. I'll watch him for a little while.' So, I sat and then I started thinking of this song and then I walked for quite a long time. I was telling the other women, 'Oh, there's a lyrebird here' and they said, 'Oh we haven't seen any,' and I said 'no, no, there is, there's so many!'

"Then the next day I thought I'd just get up again and go. So, I got up, and that same lyrebird was in the same spot and I thought 'I'll follow him this time'. It was this really steep mountain' Jo laughs as she tells me and gestures with her hands the way she was walking up the hill.

"It was really rocky, and I started following him up and then I was looking for somewhere to dance, and I thought, 'I don't really want to go to the top,' so I started to traverse down, but a bit sort of sideways, still walking along,' again she gestures to show the route. Jo is certainly a dancer and perhaps that is why she explains so much of what she is saying with her hands and movements as she speaks. Of course, it is something we all, do, but I notice how much it adds to the story.

"So, he kept popping up and I was like, 'Oh! I'm still following you!' So, then I arrived at this spot and thought 'Oh this is it, this is beautiful.' There were these really big rocks and I just started making the dance in the scrub, and I was scratching it out and I was singing the song and then I got really tired. And I mean..." she gestures to me, and places her hands on her thighs, leaning forward.

"You've learnt that lyrebird dance and it's really like, when you're doing it a lot, it's like, thigh burn! So, I'd been doing this for an hour, my thighs were a bit shaky and I thought, 'oh I'll go and put my hands on the rock, and just, you know...' she places her hands to her forehead as though they are the rock. She closes her eyes and takes a deep breath. Through the gesture she shows me a connection to the rock, and to the place. Something of the energy of the connection is communicated and it is hard to put into words, but the deep connection to place that she felt in that moment is spoken perfectly in her gesture.

"I wanted to rest my forehead because you get that beautiful... kind of... ah... you know... like if you hug a tree and you get that kind of... just that energy that goes into your third eye... So, I thought, 'I'll just put my hands on the rock, and place my head there,' and I did that and... 'oh my gosh!' Now, her movement was to move her head and neck as though looking around a corner or past something. It explained that she had seen something beyond where she was that surprised her. Her eyes widen in surprise and she looks at me and smiles.

"There was an ochre-cave. There was a hole in the wall, and it was full of sandstone and ochre. So, then I just finished the dance and the song there. And then, after that, there was just an abundance of lyrebirds, coming for the song and the dance."

The connection between dance, land, belonging and balance is clear in the way Jo expressed it. She had felt drawn to explore the land and the Lyrebird had found her and in a special way, taken her to a place where the dance could be created. She was then offered a gift of the connection with the stone and the hidden cave, as well as an abundance of Lyrebirds. Such a special story, but not only did she explain the creation of the dance and how the land spoke to her and responded to her 'work', somehow in the telling of it, she had also explained how much can be expressed in gesture with every hand movement, every facial expression, every sigh... I am incredibly grateful to be able to learn from her, and for everything she shares with our community. Being able to share in dancing the Earth like this is a treasure like no other.

The Power of the Circle

In many neo-Pagan and Earth-based spiritual practices, the sacred meeting place of the circle has become a powerful place for not only ritual, but the creation and maintenance of story. The circle itself has become a mnemonic device of sorts, holding information about the elements, the times of day and night, moon phases, seasons, agricultural celebrations, and stories of deity. In some ways we could argue it is the oral culture of modern Paganism.

The origins of the practice of coming together in a circle surely stretch back to the origins of humanity as we gathered around campfires or a meal to talk and share. I dare say there is not one place on Earth where people do not gather in a circle at times to share stories, songs and give thanks for their food, health and wellbeing. It is a natural way for us to come together and share, but in Modern neo-Pagan practice it has become much more than a casual way to hold space for each other. It has come to be a way of holding information about our connection with the land.

There is some variance in how the circle might be used from one tradition to another, and it can change depending on our location in the world. For example, there are differences between the Northern Hemisphere and Southern Hemisphere in terms of the way the elements are placed around the circle, the way the sun and moon swing across the sky and, therefore, define how we move around the circle, and the timing of the seasons in the year are associated with the circle too and the seasons are placed differently as a result of our location. These shift the ways we understand the circle on a local level, but there is still a commonality in its use as a mnemonic device.

I'll explain my own, and perhaps you can explore from here the differences between how I do it and how you might do it where you live.

I enter the circle from the western side, the place of the water element, the otherworlds and ancestors, dreams, emotions and the source of wisdom, a place representing autumn, sunset and the time of our lives as elders. I walk sunwise (anti-clockwise as I'm in the Southern Hemisphere) around the circle's inner edge past the southernmost point, the place of darkness, the Earth element, the depths of winter and midnight and place of death and rebirth. I move around to the east side, imagining the dawn shifting into daylight, the warmth coming to spring... I pause at the eastern side, and though it is midday right now, I salute the east, a place I associate with the rising sun, the springtime, youth and beauty, the element of Air, and the Goddesses Brigid and Cerridwen who initiate new beginnings, bring wisdom and inspire the poetic arts in us.

I raise my hands and imagine that energy as bringing a blessing to my circle. I'm reminded in that moment of the stories of the goddesses and gods, of the meaning and significance of springtime as a time of courting and love. I lower my hands in reverence and walk the edge of the circle once more, passing the northernmost point and place of the Fire element, summer solstice, midday, fullness of light, abundance, and growth. A place associated with adulthood, parenthood, and wholeness, but also with a recognition that with a peak comes a decline as from here the day and the year turn back again towards the depths.

Moving back to the west, I have passed each point on the circle. I speak an Acknowledgement of the Country I stand on and the Elders past and present and then call for peace to the directions. I move to the north of the circle and call for peace to the ranges and forests there, to the cities and towns where people live and countries far across the sea. I raise my arms and send out my hope for peace in all beings there in the words: "may there be peace in the north." I move to the south and imagine the places in that direction: "may there be peace in the south," and then to the west and east the same. In each place I ask that there be peace for all in those directions, coming to an awareness of the location of my circle in space between them all.

Moving to each place and raising my arms again, I call to the elements in the quarters:

"I call to the east and the element of Air; to the sulphur crested cockatoo with rays of Awen streaming from your bright brow; to the magpie's song at dawn; and to the keen eye of the hawk that flies high in the vault of blue. I call to Brigid, lady of poets, let my mind be clear, my words eloquent, my ideas keen. May the element of Air bless my ritual today with clarity, focus and the art of the bards. Hail and welcome.

"I call to the north and the element of Fire; to the wisdom of the red bellied black snake; to the call of the red-tailed black cockatoo; to the red kangaroo and emu. I call to the fires of summer sun, and regenerative bushfire to bring life, abundance, passion, energy and love, in warming balance to my ritual today. Hail and welcome.

"I call to the west and the element of Water; to the great rivers and floodplains, to the ancient Murray cod and crocodile; to the whale and dolphin of the western seas. Bring today wisdom of the source, in creativity, love and emotion. Let my ritual today be blessed with water's flow and nourishment. Hail and welcome.

"I call to the south and the element of Earth; to the wombat deep in her burrow; to the nests of ants deep in the soil; to the roots of trees that wind their way through rock and sand seeking nourishment. Bring today knowledge of presence, wisdom through the senses, and a grounding in the wonders of form. Let my ritual today be blessed with Earth's strength, and healing stillness. Hail and welcome."

I acknowledge the ancestors of my bloodline, my inspirations, and the land. I meditate for a moment, moving into my senses of sight, hearing, touch, taste and smell. I acknowledge the season: a particular point on the circle will hold the place of the season, like a clock of the year that begins with winter in the south, moving the spring in the east, summer in the north, and autumn in the west. Today has a place on the circle and its story will be told.

The land around me tells the story in blossoms and bird calls, in the temperature of the wind and the angle of the sun, in the availability of flowers, fruits or nuts in the garden and orchard – each place on the circle seeming to hold them within it.

The circle tells stories of our lives as we are born, grow, mature, become elders, and pass away, death and birth holding the same space, alluding to a belief in reincarnation, as though we will live again and again, just like the seasons of the Earth, the hours of the day, and the turning of the wheel.

The circle tells all the stories of life and each point on it holds more than could ever be told.

Garden Life

Becoming a part of the land we live in, and serving it as it serves us, is usually done with small actions of love. I started volunteering at the Blue Mountains Organic Community Gardens a few months before the fires started in 2019, soon after my trip to the rivers. I had attended sporadically for a few months and took some time off when the smoke had been too thick to be outside much. I enjoyed my time there but didn't really commit to it until the winter of 2020 when we found ourselves just emerging from the lockdown of the Covid-19 pandemic. It was then that I appreciated how good it was for me to be there, and how much of a difference my two little hands could make there.

Lockdown had really taken its toll on me emotionally. The fires had been hard enough over the summer of 2019/2020 and, as autumn began in March, we got some heavy rain that caused landslides and took out the local train line. Katoomba is a little tourist town in the mountains and the fires, then floods, and the train line being knocked out had really hurt local businesses. We could hardly believe it when the pandemic hit, and we had to go into lockdown. I wasn't sure I could take it. I had to cancel various trips I had planned; home-schooling began and we were stuck in the house for a few months. To be honest, we have been incredibly lucky in Australia compared to other countries, and today I count my blessings as life is emerging shyly into a semblance of normality, though poised to batten down the hatches again at the slightest sign of a threat.

At that time though, coming out of lockdown in May and June 2020, I felt emotionally devastated and the gardens seemed to reflect how I was feeling. My emotional state was directly linked to what was happening in the world around me. It felt like it was all falling apart, and myself with it. I had hardly had time to process the fires, let alone get my head around the effects of this global health issue and what the consequences of it could be going forward. There didn't seem to be an end in sight then. Even now, we're only just catching glimpses of it. I was at a really low point and wasn't feeling ready even for ritual, but the gardens offered a window of hope.

The first day I went down there, it was July. It was a sunny day, but it was cold. For the first hour or so I just walked around and saw what had become of it while we had all been in lockdown and hiding away from the smoke and fires. The grass had grown long. The vegetable patches were overgrown with weeds. Some trees still held onto leaves badly damaged by the smoke. There were projects half-finished and areas needing a lot of attention. The gardens, like me, looked battered about by the harsh world we were living through. I felt a knot in my throat as I realised that I felt much the same as these beautiful sorry little plants.

There was so much to do, I didn't know where to start. I wandered in the food forest and noticed a pile of old bricks in amongst the leaves. I bent down and started to lay them out as though marking the edge of a pathway through the trees. I kept at it slowly, and was surprised when my friend Michael, who also volunteers at the gardens, also turned up. We decided to make the path together, we found our enthusiasm and moved some mulch over it, lining the sides with the old bricks. Within an hour or two we had made an old pile of bricks and a pile of wood chip mulch transform a little part of the forest into a lovely pathway. In a few hours our work had made a difference, and we felt better in ourselves too.

The simple joy that came from that day is hard to describe. It healed my heart of the heavy sadness that had been on it. It eased the frown that had burrowed its way into my brow through staring too long at screens full of bad news. There was something indescribably healing and good about spending time in the garden. And as we returned week after week, we weeded the garden beds, trimmed back the damaged leaves, finished the projects left undone, and felt ourselves become healed a little more with every action. More people joined us and we shared a sense of community, getting together to make a difference in our world in small but meaningful ways.

I grabbed my hat and tugged on my gum boots. It was gardening day. I packed the car with some empty pots, a big basket and a bit of bread and cheese that I could add a handful of herbs and salad leaves to from the gardens for lunch. It is only a little way down the road but I know I will have some apples and potatoes to bring home today as it is late summer and they are heavy to carry home.

I park the car and head over to the mudbrick sheds that were built by a permaculture community group in the late nineties. I unlock the doors and put the kettle on. My friend Louise arrives and we have a chat about our week. We make tea and settle on the log chairs outside as more of our friends turn up. We have a chat about what we might like to do with our day. Louise is going to work on the medicinal garden, and Michael has plans to trim some of the branches over the pathways. I think I will cut back the blackberry on the swale banks so that we can put in a native flower garden.

Each week there is plenty to do, but we don't make many plans. We always start with a cuppa and the jobs present themselves as our moods take us. It might be harvesting some vegies, planting natives along the creek, or fixing up the mosaics on our labyrinth. It could be tidying up the meeting area, picking weeds, working on the compost, planting some seeds or moving mulch around – there is always something to do. As we work, we talk about plants and the seasons, we notice the birds and other creatures that come to visit, and life slows down into that quiet space where conversations become more contemplative. Thoughts have room to wander and there is time to tell stories of our lives as we rummage around for a potato or trim back the comfrey for the compost heap.

Plans emerge and ideas for what the gardens could bring in the future are formed. We hear the history of the place from those who remember, and meet new people who have ideas and energy to bring in something new. The hours fly by and by the end, with a basket full of potatoes, herbs, flowers, apples, blackberries and artichokes – more than I'd thought I was coming for – I feel like I could be here every day.

Every few weeks we get together for a seasonal circle. About ten to fifteen of us stand in the circle of stones and talk about the changes we've noticed. The land moves with us. We are a part of this place. We tend to her and she tends to us, heals us. We grow together, whatever challenges we face.

Gardens are healing places. Alongside work comes food, friendship and peace, connection and abundance. And not only that – we are also contributing to a beautiful community space that can be enjoyed by anyone and everyone, and get to eat food from the land that never had to be packaged or transported across vast distances, bought and sold, and grown with chemicals that damage the earth. It's all just here, and free and full of goodness and abundance.

Living Earth Wisdom

Whether we are talking about Druidry, the psychology of ecological activism, or Indigenous cultures of First Nations people, nature-based spiritual practices are deeply concerned with how humans are a part of the Earth. Our responsibilities towards the Earth, our love for her as a mother to us, and the way that our inner states reflect the world around us are a consequence of deep connection. A connection that brings us pain and hardship when the Earth is in need, and one that brings joy and abundance when the world comes back into balance. This is what it means to be a part of the Earth, and what it means to truly belong here. We are the Earth because we feel as she feels. We are threatened when she is threatened. We grieve with her when she is in pain. Yet we also heal with her when we recognise this.

In this book, I have shared stories of finding connection to place – my own and those of others. As we explore the troubles the Earth faces, and as we learn more about how we can all do better, we help the Earth and ourselves to heal. We find ourselves today in times of great change and challenge, and it can feel overwhelming when we consider how much needs to be rectified and brought to balance, but in small acts of love, ritual, art, poetry, making friends, listening and being respectful to Indigenous cultures of the land, we can be the change we want to see in the world. We can become more aware of the importance of our connection with the Earth.

I wish you every blessing on your path ahead and hope that these stories inspire you to find your own stories of connection and share stories with others, for each of us belongs to Mother Earth. Each of us has ancestors that hold us with their stories and connections. Each of us lives in a place full of history, nature and wisdom. Even if the world is changing around us, we can connect in the present moment, knowing that we too are changing, that we are affected by the environment we are a part of and belong to and that we can make a difference through our acts of love and connection. This is how we respond to a world in crisis because this is how we should always respond to the Earth – as a part of her, responsible for her, and to her, grateful for all she gives us in return.

About the Author

Julie Brett is the founder of Druids Down Under, an online networking group for those studying various paths in Druidry in the Southern Hemisphere and particularly Australia. She is also the author of *Australian Druidry: Connecting with the Sacred Landscape* 2017 Moon Books. You can find out more about her work through her website www.juliebrett.net

Bibliography

Daniel, Sarah, Sara Judge, Gareth Thomas (eds.), *Listening to Land: A poetic action against the raising of the Warragamba dam wall*, 2019, IngramSpark: Tennessee

Wall Kimmerer, Robin, *Braiding Sweetgrass: Indigenous Wisdom, Scientific Knowledge, and the Teaching of Plants*, 2013, Milkweed Editions: Minneapolis

Johnson, Dianne, in collaboration with the residents of the Gully and their descendants, *Sacred Waters: The Story of the Blue Mountains Gully Traditional Owners*, 2007, Halstead Press: Broadway

Johnson, Trebbe, *Radical Joy for Hard Times: Finding meaning and Making Beauty in Earth's Broken Places"*, 2018, North Atlantic Books: Berkeley

Neale, Margo (Ed.), *Songlines: Tracking the Seven Sisters*, 2017, National Museum of Australia Press: Canberra

Pascoe, Bruce, *Dark Emu: Black Seeds: agriculture or accident?* 2014, Magabala Books Aboriginal Corporation: Broome

Seed, John; Joanna Macy; Pat Flemming; Arne Naess, *Thinking Like a Mountain: Towards a council of All Beings*, 1988 (2007), New Catalyst Books: Gabriola Island

Suzuki, David, *The Sacred Balance: Rediscovering our Place in Nature*, 1997 (2007), The David Suzuki Foundation: Vancouver

Other books in the *Earth Spirit* series

Confronting the Crisis
Essays and Meditations on Eco-Spirituality
David Sparenberg
978-1-78904-973-2 (Paperback)
978-1-78904-974-9 (ebook)

Eco-Spirituality and Human–Animal Relationships
Through an Ethical and Spiritual Lens
Mark Hawthorne
978-1-78535-248-5 (Paperback)
978-1-78535-249-2 (ebook)

Environmental Gardening
Think Global Act Local
Elen Sentier
978-1-78904-963-3 (Paperback)
978-1-78904-964-0 (ebook)

Healthy Planet
Global Meltdown or Global Healing
Fred Hageneder
978-1-78904-830-8 (Paperback)
978-1-78904-831-5 (ebook)

Honoring the Wild
Reclaiming Witchcraft and Environmental Activism
Irisanya Moon
978-1-78904-961-9 (Paperback)
978-1-78904-962-6 (ebook)

Saving Mother Ocean
We all need to help save the seas!
Steve Andrews
978-1-78904-965-7 (Paperback)
978-1-78904-966-4 (ebook)

The Circle of Life is Broken
An Eco-Spiritual Philosophy of the Climate Crisis
Brendan Myers
978-1-78904-977-0 (Paperback)
978-1-78904-978-7 (ebook)

MOON
BOOKS

PAGANISM & SHAMANISM

What is Paganism? A religion, a spirituality, an alternative
belief system, nature worship? You can find support for all these
definitions (and many more) in dictionaries, encyclopaedias, and
text books of religion, but subscribe to any one and the truth will
evade you. Above all Paganism is a creative pursuit, an encounter
with reality, an exploration of meaning and an expression of the
soul. Druids, Heathens, Wiccans and others, all contribute their
insights and literary riches to the Pagan tradition. Moon Books
invites you to begin or to deepen your own encounter, right here,
right now.

If you have enjoyed this book, why not tell other readers by
posting a review on your preferred book site.

Recent bestsellers from Moon Books are:

Journey to the Dark Goddess
How to Return to Your Soul
Jane Meredith
Discover the powerful secrets of the Dark Goddess and
transform your depression, grief and pain into healing
and integration.
Paperback: 978-1-84694-677-6 ebook: 978-1-78099-223-5

Shamanic Reiki
Expanded Ways of Working with Universal Life Force Energy
Llyn Roberts, Robert Levy
Shamanism and Reiki are each powerful ways of healing; together,
their power multiplies. *Shamanic Reiki* introduces techniques to
help healers and Reiki practitioners tap ancient healing wisdom.
Paperback: 978-1-84694-037-8 ebook: 978-1-84694-650-9

Pagan Portals – The Awen Alone
Walking the Path of the Solitary Druid
Joanna van der Hoeven
An introductory guide for the solitary Druid, *The Awen Alone* will
accompany you as you explore, and seek out your own place
within the natural world.
Paperback: 978-1-78279-547-6 ebook: 978-1-78279-546-9

A Kitchen Witch's World of Magical Herbs & Plants
Rachel Patterson
A journey into the magical world of herbs and plants, filled with
magical uses, folklore, history and practical magic. By popular
writer, blogger and kitchen witch, Tansy Firedragon.
Paperback: 978-1-78279-621-3 ebook: 978-1-78279-620-6

Medicine for the Soul
The Complete Book of Shamanic Healing
Ross Heaven
All you will ever need to know about shamanic healing and how to
become your own shaman...
Paperback: 978-1-78099-419-2 ebook: 978-1-78099-420-8

Shaman Pathways – The Druid Shaman
Exploring the Celtic Otherworld
Danu Forest
A practical guide to Celtic shamanism with exercises and
techniques as well as traditional lore for exploring the Celtic
Otherworld.
Paperback: 978-1-78099-615-8 ebook: 978-1-78099-616-5

Traditional Witchcraft for the Woods and Forests
A Witch's Guide to the Woodland with Guided Meditations and
Pathworking
Mélusine Draco
A Witch's guide to walking alone in the woods, with guided
meditations and pathworking.
Paperback: 978-1-84694-803-9 ebook: 978-1-84694-804-6

Wild Earth, Wild Soul
A Manual for an Ecstatic Culture
Bill Pfeiffer
Imagine a nature-based culture so alive and so connected,
spreading like wildfire. This book is the first flame...
Paperback: 978-1-78099-187-0 ebook: 978-1-78099-188-7

Naming the Goddess
Trevor Greenfield
Naming the Goddess is written by over eighty adherents and
scholars of Goddess and Goddess Spirituality.
Paperback: 978-1-78279-476-9 ebook: 978-1-78279-475-2

Shapeshifting into Higher Consciousness
Heal and Transform Yourself and Our World with Ancient
Shamanic and Modern Methods
Llyn Roberts
Ancient and modern methods that you can use every day to
transform yourself and make a positive difference in the world.
Paperback: 978-1-84694-843-5 ebook: 978-1-84694-844-2

Readers of ebooks can buy or view any of these bestsellers by
clicking on the live link in the title. Most titles are published in
paperback and as an ebook. Paperbacks are available in traditional
bookshops. Both print and ebook formats are available online.

Find more titles and sign up to our readers' newsletter at
http://www.johnhuntpublishing.com/paganism
Follow us on Facebook at https://www.facebook.com/MoonBooks
and Twitter at https://twitter.com/MoonBooksJHP